WHY BELIEVE WHEN
YOU CAN KNOW?

Alan Valiant

Published by the author.

PRINTED IN GREAT BRITAIN BY BPCC WHEATONS LTD, EXETER

Other work by Alan Valiant:

How to Talk with the Dead, 1987

My Conversations with Jesus Christ, 1989

Editor of A Course in Spiritual Philosophy

by Madam Amanda Valiant, 1991

Masculine pronouns have been used almost
exclusively throughout the text for
euphony. Where it is obvious that the
feminine gender is also implied, this
should be read into the text, as no
invalidation is intended by its
omission.

Acknowledgements

I extend my grateful thanks to God,
Jesus Christ and all other High
Spiritual Beings Who have helped
in giving me much of the information
contained in this book.

My special thanks go to my late
wife, Amanda, for making this work
possible and to Dr Eli Feldman of
New York for his encouragement and
loyal support.

CONTENTS

FOREWORD

At last, the Truth about existence has been revealed, free from all mysticism and religious prejudice. Now that the knowledge is available to all, belief is unnecessary.

The information disclosed in this book may shock many but many more will welcome it because, never in the history of man on earth, have the facts of being been fully explained by the hierarchy in the spiritual universe through incarnate psychics.

In the following pages, you will learn what Jesus Christ thinks of Christianity today and the truth about His birth, life and death and the Purpose behind His last incarnation on earth. You will discover who Jesus Christ really is and His present position in heaven.

We are all on earth for a purpose and you will learn what that purpose is and what you must do to raise yourself spiritually. The facts about sin and its effects are elucidated.

You will find out what happens to the famous benefactors and the infamous malefactors after they die. "There are many paths to God" is an often-quoted cliché but the fact is that there is only one basic path to the condition of high spirituality and an understanding of God.

All religions are blind alleys and those who travel the paths laid down by the churches find themselves, eventually, having to retrace their steps in order to seek anew the true path. Only if you have courage should you continue to read this book because the truth about yourself may shock you. There is an old saw, "The truth hurts!" It is a valid saying. Most of us live our lives in a smug, self-complacent manner, oblivious of our spiritual past and not wishing to know it for fear of retribution. After we die, however, there is no escape and all the good and the evil are laid before us. The laws that govern human destiny are inexorable. Goethe wrote, "If anyone advances anything new which contradicts, perhaps threatens to overturn, what we have for years repeated and have handed down to others, all passions are raised against him and every effort is made to crush him. People resist with all their might; they act as if they neither heard nor could comprehend; they speak of the new view with contempt, as if it were not worth the trouble of even an investigation or a regard, and thus a new truth may wait a long time before it can make its way."

By my own observations, those who are the most vehement and bitterly sceptical of spiritual phenomena have had no personal experience of them. They misevaluate the work of others who, having received ample evidence during a long period of time, often find it impossible adequately to convey the substance of their experience to others. Unfortunately, it is instinctive in the "believer" to evaluate any evidence that contradicts his belief from a point of view of knowing nothing about it. The devout are incapable, in general, of assessing spiritual evidence rationally and yet their entire faith may be founded upon the abundance of spiritual events in the bible.

Any person who carries out a sincere, open-minded investigation into psychic phenomena will, eventually, become convinced of their reality. Those who persist in denying the evidence, either deliberately conceal the facts through bigotry or are genuinely ignorant of them.

1

Some scientists, who once opposed vigourously the work of their colleagues in psychic investigations, have been honest enough to admit their folly after their own studies forced them to admit the evidence. No attempt is made in this work to PROVE anything with regard to the spiritual existence. The proof may be obtained in a variety of ways from numerous other sources either by direct, personal experience or through spiritual mediums of many different kinds. As a teacher of spiritual knowledge, I do not give "sittings" to those who are merely curious or who wish to communicate with their departed friends and relatives. There are others who specialise in this form of mediumship and it is they who should be consulted if confirmation of the continuation of life after death is desired.

My late wife, Amanda, and I described the spiritual state as it actually is. Our work brought us into communication with High Spiritual Beings every day of our lives and I still enjoy this great privilege. We not only have their descriptions of their own lives in heaven written through us but were also able to astral travel to the higher planes and see for ourselves the true nature of the next world, to meet in their own environment those who helped us daily and to experience, at first hand, the splendour and grandeur of the realms of spirit. Throughout history, every man who, through the application of his intelligence, acquired an understanding of a subject of which others were ignorant, or who claimed to have invented a device of the utmost importance to mankind, was scorned and ridiculed by the public and, frequently, his own colleagues.

Galileo, the seventeenth-century astronomer, was ordered by the pope to appear before the Inquisition, where he was tortured until he recanted his theory that the sun was the central body around which the earth and the other planets revolved. Galileo was right!

When Marco Polo, on his return to Europe, claimed that there were black stones in China which would burn, he was ridiculed. Nowadays, coal is of vital importance.

Alexander Graham Bell's invention of the telephone was considered to be an insane idea. How could anyone possibly speak to somebody along a mile of wire? Some believed that his invention could never be of practical use and that, even if it could, its best place would be in a side-show. No-one ridicules telephones any more.

Marconi was derided when he said he would send messages across the Atlantic. Just consider the extent of radio coverage, now!

In the seventeenth century, William Harvey discovered the blood circulation system but his medical colleagues, in their jealous ignorance, poured scorn on his theories and he died, still defending his knowledge. He was right, as history has shown, and every modern cardiologist is indebted to him.

We accept as normal today that which was ridiculed by myopic "experts" of the past. The false, self-assurance of many people is nothing less than arrogance, and professional jealousy has always been a barrier to progress.

At the present time, numerous examples of previous-life experiences are brought before the public through the various media. Tape recordings by hypnotherapists contain some excellent examples of anamnesis but the learned deny that we live more than once and psychiatrists flounder in a sea of jargon.

2

It is the habit of some writers concerned with metaphysical subjects to over-complicate what are, basically, simple concepts. Elementary principles are wrapped up in the language of religion or psychology and presented in such a prolix manner that few, if any, readers can comprehend the author's meanings. The author deliberately sets out to display his erudition by blinding people with science but usually falls into the time-worn traps of dogma and current scientific opinion.

No small wonder that philosophy is virtually an incomprehensible subject even to the learned university fraternity. What they think they know, they do not know.

More than one speculator on the occult and metaphysical has remarked that, one day, a breakthrough would be made to the Highermost. Amanda and I have made the breakthrough.

In pursuing knowledge for the benefit of mankind, we have broken down the barriers of the unknown and have opened new spiritual frontiers.

INTRODUCTION

The mysteries of my own existence, having been in the forefront of my mind all my life, have been the subject of much contemplation. I reasoned that at some future time, presumably after death, all would be revealed but I realised that it was extremely difficult to find a source of true information while incarnate. The "isms", "ologies", cults and religions all vying for supremacy were, to me, barking up the wrong tree. One or two plausible theories cropped up occasionally but, on the whole, no hypostasis that I ever came across had the ring of truth.

Meanwhile, I was accumulating more and more experience through my own suffering and by attempting to alleviate the emotional sufferings of others. It became more than mere coincidence that men and women would take me completely into their confidence, on occasions after having only just met me. They would confide in me and pour out their troubles as though they had known me for years.

Because I had suffered terrible emotional stress myself and had subsequently climbed back to full health, I found that I could help others through their crises and numerous people in dire need of spiritual help were brought my way. I know, now, that they were guided to me and I have, long ago, ceased to believe in coincidence. Having seen people pull themselves out of their distress after I had shown them the way, I began to understand the real, hidden causes of emotional trauma.

All the while, I pondered upon the possible nature of the life after this one. I knew with certainty that one survived but in what kind of environment I could not, then, understand.

Without my having any suspicions, my behaviour and my thoughts had not passed unnoticed by certain highly-placed spiritual beings in heaven but I was not to discover this for several more years.

My first marriage having ended in divorce, after a disastrous period attempting to raise my son and daughter in an ethical manner against impossible odds, I was earnestly seeking a partner whom I could love and who would love me in return.

Six years after the separation, I had still not met a woman with whom I had any affinity or who had anything in common with me. The kind of wife that I sought was one who would be able to share at least some of my many interests. Relying on a "chance" meeting with a prospective wife turned out to be a fruitless approach and, since I knew exactly the kind of partner that I sought, I was very particular.

Finally, a casual meeting with a young Israeli gave me the prompt that I needed. Having enjoyed an intellectual discussion with him, I confessed that all I really lacked in life was love. At that the young man said, "Well, why are you standing here talking to me? You must go where women go!"

After a few days letting this sink in, I decided to go to a dance hall. It was not that I really enjoyed dancing; as a musician, I have always preferred to play in the band but that seemed to be a logical place to attract a member of the opposite sex. However, the event proved unavailing and I returned home disappointed. Thinking that perhaps my dancing was below par, I decided to take some lessons. Thumbing through the Yellow Pages in the telephone directory, I found

4

a list of several dancing schools. One of the names stood out as though illuminated and, as I scanned the list, my eyes repeatedly fell upon that particular name. That day, I made the decision to go for a trial dancing lesson.

The evening was interesting enough and passed pleasantly but I was not really impressed with the ladies present. It was difficult to decide whether to go again or to give up. In the event, I decided to try once more. On this occasion, I danced with and conversed with a lady to whom my company seemed to bring pleasure. We met for dancing lessons several times after that and became very attached to each other.

My new-found friend's name was Amanda. It was not long before we found that we had one very important thing in common; we shared a deep interest in the spiritual existence and we had both had experience that convinced us of the existence of the spiritual world. Although we had each had to endure Sunday school and church-going as children, the experience had only left us bereft of understanding as to the supposed benefits of such activities.

Instinctively, we knew that the answers to life's riddles were plainer and simpler than those offered by the Christian religions. With so much in common, it was inevitable that we became man and wife.

For the next five years, my work took up all my time as I was often working seven days a week. Living in our cramped, rented accommodation was wearing us down and Amanda, seeing an advertisement in a newspaper, suggested that we investigate a flat that was being offered.

Upon arrival at the site, we were delighted at the remote situation and the charm of the ancient country mansion in which we were offered a spacious suite with a beautiful view of the countryside from the living room windows. We moved in.

After a time, the pressures of my work subsided a little and Amanda and I, feeling more able to relax, still often discussed existence and other aspects of metaphysics. The peaceful, silent atmosphere was highly conducive to the development of psychic powers yet, at the time, neither of us suspected that we had any. Sitting quietly in our pleasant living room, we became aware of other "presences". Then, we both began to receive communications by spirit writing. After merely holding a pen to paper, our hands would write. At first, the communications were unintelligible but, after some days, sensible messages appeared before our eyes.

Every day, a spiritual being would write through us. At first, our deceased relatives came and chatted to us. We soon discovered that they could read our thoughts and we did not need to speak aloud. Of course, we asked numerous questions and were greatly intrigued by some of the answers.

By the end of a month, our ability to converse with those in the "other world" had reached a high standard. My guide, Abe, had made himself known to me and had given me some priceless information. I was advised to read certain library books, the titles of which were given to me. Although I had never heard of the books or their authors, I located the books as requested. This gave me a very strong reality on the authenticity of my spiritual informants.

It was not long before I discovered that, if a spiritual being came

5

into my room, I was aware of his name telepathically. It was in this way that I was introduced to Malcolm Campbell. Sitting quietly, resting, I suddenly said to myself, "Malcolm Campbell is here." Then, I picked up paper and pencil and he immediately confirmed that he was, indeed, there. Similarly, a few days later, I said to myself, "Albert Schweitzer is here", and promptly began a conversation with him.

Shortly after discovering that I could receive telepathic messages directly from spiritual beings, I noticed that I could even see them. Vague in form and outline, at first, they appeared more real and solid as the days passed. Their movements became observable to me and I could see whether they were standing or sitting. Describing the garments of our spiritual visitors became a daily routine and I was soon able to see the colours of their robes and to describe the ornaments that they wore such as a medallion suspended from a chain around the neck, popular amongst High Spiritual Beings.

One day, a new means of communication was revealed to me. As my psychic vision was now extremely good, for important, formal messages, the High Spiritual Being would, sometimes, unroll a scroll, vertically. After concentrating on the writing on it, I found that I could read it. The writing is always in concept script which is the universal written language in heaven. It can be understood by anyone. The books in the great libraries on each plane are written in concept script.

Within a few months, Amanda and I had developed our psychic awareness to a considerable degree. We had become clairaudient to the extent that we could hear Albert Schweitzer playing his organ and also the laughter of our spiritual friends.

Up to this point, we had no inkling of the amazing task that lay ahead of us nor of the astounding knowledge with which we were soon to be entrusted.

Amanda, without my knowledge, had been secretly communicating with God for some time but she was asked by Him not to tell me. Then, later, God decided that, as Jesus Christ had already written through me, He, God, would also reveal Himself to me. From then on, God communicated with me also but only through Amanda. I was, apparently, still on trial to see how I would react to the amazing revelatory events that occurred each passing day. Finally, God wrote through my hand directly when Amanda was otherwise occupied.

It was revealed that Amanda had been reincarnated, at her own request, in order to carry out a most important task involving bringing the abilities and powers of those in the spiritual world to the notice of people on earth in yet one more attempt to convince them that they are not alone and that help is always forthcoming from heaven, if they have deserved it. Her original purpose was thwarted, though, by ignorant and suppressive people who, through adherence to their own self-interests, ruined her kharma.

Amanda was informed by God that He had watched her closely, all her life, and had even intervened to save her from accident while driving her car, on two occasions, in addition to protecting her from danger during air raids on three different towns during the second world war. God was deeply concerned that Amanda had been prevented from fulfilling her intended kharma.

It was at this stage that Amanda was communicated with by the

leader of the hierarchy in heaven and informed that she was a member
of that hierarchy. Intensively trained by the Gardeners of the Earth
who constitute the government in heaven, Amanda had returned to earth
to carry out the task for which she had volunteered. She belongs to
Sphere Eight where she now works with the Lord God. Amanda returned to
heaven on 4th November 1988, after a heart attack at the age of sixty-
three years.

There may be some people who believe, through their religious
indoctrination, that if Amanda is so spiritually high, then she should
be able to perform miracles. This is an erroneous conception because
although through her knowledge she has worked wonders in helping
others, she does not produce apports or materialise objects or make
any attempt to utilise those techniques of drawing the attention of
people to the spiritual world that find such favour on the lower
planes of existence. Because Jesus Christ had to deal largely with un-
educated people, He was endowed with ostentatious abilities in the
psychic field.

Amanda's approach was by appealing to people's intellects, for she
has a vast knowledge of the spiritual existence and, particularly, of
her own past lives.

I consider myself the luckiest man on this planet to have been
chosen to help Amanda recover something from the ashes of her final
incarnation which had resulted from the appalling treatment that she
received at the hands of others. First, I used my knowledge and
experience to the full in order to help her re-establish herself as a
person. So effectively had she been suppressed that she had lost faith
in herself and had retreated into a condition in which she could no
longer confront life.

The beneficial results of my efforts soon began to show and,
gradually, Amanda started to face up to life and people with a
confidence and vigour that she had never, previously, shown.
Apparently, I was the first man she had met socially who did not
attempt to belittle her or exploit her.

After we both came into the knowledge of the truth, our lives were
transformed. We were able to communicate every day, at any time we
wished, with many of our numerous spiritual friends including God and
Jesus Christ for whom we have the deepest love and respect. Knowing
who we were and where we shall be after we return to heaven had
brought us to the realisation that the life AFTER death is, if one has
fulfilled one's kharma well, infinitely superior to the troubled
existence that most of earth's inhabitants experience.

We were both aware that we were being kept on earth for the sole
purpose of spreading the truth that we had been given to as wide a
public as possible, since these were the wishes of God and the
Gardeners of the earth.

Having visited the highest planes in heaven by astral travelling,
we were privileged to have glimpsed the glorious, most beautiful state
in which High Spiritual Beings live and which will be our future
domain.

The wit, integrity, composure and instantaneous willingness to help
us and others expressed by our highly spiritual friends indicate, very
forcefully, the advantages of life after death on the higher planes.

My own soul-mate, Tena, is, apart from being one hundred percent compatible with me, the most vivacious personality that I have ever come across and, although she has been "dead" for about two hundred and forty years, she is more alive than anyone on earth. Her mind is totally alert and she reacts instantly to every question or statement. If only people on earth could communicate as she does, there would be an end to strife.

Gradually, by virtue of the great help that I received from Amanda, my own spiritual state began to improve. There were many surprises and even shocks in store for me when I was confronted by my own akashic record. First of all, I was told by Jesus Christ, through Amanda, something about my earlier lives with her, for this is the fourth time that we have come together in different lives.

Later, I was taken in my spiritual body to Plane Four to see my akashic record in the Great Hall of Memories. So upsetting was this experience, in view of my awful behaviour in several earlier lives, that I was left in a state of shock. It was explained to me by Jesus Christ that I could not rise any higher spiritually unless I were willing to confront my own past and accept total responsibility for it.

Because the most important questions in my life had been metaphysical ones, I agreed to lay my soul bare. There seemed to be little point in behaving in any other way since it was obvious that not only God but Jesus Christ and many other High Spiritual Beings knew everything there was to know about me in all my incarnations.

Admittedly, this revealing of one's innermost thoughts and actions is a painful process but it was pointed out to me that the only way up the spiritual scale is through the "wall of fire". This is an apt phrase because most people shrink from confronting their own past in the same way as they would back away from flames.

After I had recovered from the initial shock of seeing my behaviour in several former incarnations, I was shown some of the more pleasant aspects of my previous existence. It was a great relief to know that I had not always been wicked and that I had had some successful lives in which I had advanced my kharma significantly.

At no time did Amanda or I witness any of the spiritualistic types of phenomena that are so often the subject of derision and suspicion amongst the public. So certain did we become of our sources of information and so adept at communication and astral travelling that we found ourselves living a large portion of our lives in the spiritual world.

Materialisations were not necessary in order to convince us of the reality of our work and the most corroborative evidence of the truth of our mutual experiences was the fact that we each developed our psychic abilities in parallel, confirming one another's observations as we progressed.

After we began teaching others, some of them also reached the stage when they could confirm our findings. Some incarnate people carry in their subconscious minds a terrible burden of guilt and it is this that restricts and limits their acceptance of the truth. In extreme cases, the seeker will react to the presentation of the truth with anger, as has the Christian church so often in the past. Unable to comprehend and preferring to adhere to dogma or the "everybody knows" syndrome, they become fearful, thinking that they are being threatened from without when in reality the only threat is from within themselves.

Scientists have begun to lose the confidence of the general public when it comes to an explanation of existence merely because they have patently demonstrated their inabilities in this field. The reverence in which science was once held by certain groups of people has waned.

The great work that science, in general, produces for the benefit of mankind is highly plausible and, when limiting their investigations to physical phenomena, they remain paramount. There is no materialistic theory of existence that can possibly possess the remotest validity, since existence is fundamentally spiritual.

Investigation of the spiritual world MUST be carried out by people capable of opening their minds and setting aside preconceptions garnered from their early training or professional teachings.

For at least a century, in modern times, spiritualist phenomena have held sway and, while they are part and parcel of the education of many people as to the reality of the life after death, they represent, in general, the frequently aberrated and ill-informed communications between low spiritual beings in heaven and on earth.

For the truth to be accepted, spiritual education must be elevated from the currently existing low levels to the highly ethical and practical standards employed by High Spiritual Beings.

It is with the greatest humility that I offer this book to the reader. Having bared my soul, literally, before God, Jesus Christ and the Gardeners of the Earth, it is impossible for me to display arrogance. Knowing the source of my information as I do, my attitude is one of tremendous relief at having achieved my life's ambition, namely, to discover the truth about existence, coupled with a deep sense of gratitude for the great honour that has been bestowed upon me by my having been chosen as an instrument or channel through whom the truth can be presented.

In return for my having helped Amanda she, and numerous High Spiritual Beings in heaven, have assisted me. During all of my activities, I receive help and guidance from those in heaven who are experts in the appropriate field of experience. Not only were these people famous in their last incarnations but they speak now from the highest vantage point, that of knowing the truth.

After all the camouflage of religion and mysticism has been removed, the truth is available and observable but, in the present spiritual climate on earth, it may be compared with attempting to find a pin dropped in a vast jungle, The mental and spiritual disarray extant today is indicative of the confusion in people's minds. Millions are avidly searching for enlightenment but, unfortunately, many are fooled by self-styled leaders whose actual knowledge is limited to say the least and who merely sell their own particular brand of "salvation".

The ONLY route to salvation is thoroughly explained in this book and no amount of jumping up and down, drug-induced hallucinations, ritual chanting and dancing will ever bring enlightenment, for this is only achievable after intensive study. Expressed in another way, the path to salvation lies through the mind and NOT through physical experiences.

CHAPTER ONE

THE NATURE OF THE SPIRITUAL UNIVERSE

In my twenties, after having read about many examples of telepathy
and other aspects of extra-sensory perception, I came to the
conclusion that there could not possibly be a physical or scientific
explanation for such phenomena. By then, I had had a few psychic
experiences of my own so that, by the age of thirty, I had made a firm
affirmation that the answers to all the enigmatic situations that did
not fit into the normal pattern of scientific theory and experience
must be of "spiritual" origin. Admittedly, I did not understand what
the word really meant until I discovered that I was able to enjoy at
will that which is now known as an out-of-body experience. In other
words, I could leave my physical body in a chair or on a bed and
wander abroad in the physical universe still, incredibly, able to see.

It soon became apparent to me that, when out of my body, I could
move through walls and roofs and, amazingly, could travel at the speed
of thought since distance, when one is in purely spiritual form, is
not a consideration.

After many years of practising the art of exteriorisation, which is
another name for the experience, I was able to move to almost anywhere
I wished in the physical universe. It was, without doubt, the
realities gained during such journeys that gave me the total
conviction that I am a spiritual being and that I do not need a body
in order to exist. Obviously, I reasoned, if I can exist away from my
body and still see and think and compute then bodies are not essential
to the existence of the personal entity.

Utterly convinced, now, that I was immortal. I began to research
subjects allied to affairs of the spirit, subjects that, earlier in
my life, I would have regarded as unrealistic. Simultaneously, I
undertook to train my mind in various ways in order to attempt to
change my life, which seemed to me in my early thirties, to be leading
nowhere.

My reading matter became any subject dealing with the spiritual
existence. There are hundreds of books available on all aspects of
life after death, out-of-body experiences, extrasensory perception,
psychic manifestations, mediumship and similar subjects.

While I read, I tried to guard against evaluating the subject
matter from the point of view of that which I thought I already
knew, Instead, I attempted to keep my mind open and never to
invalidate something if I knew little or nothing about it. However, I
had developed, over many years of study, an ability to discern the
feasible from the fanciful and, as I had done with my early religious
teachings, I instinctively rejected many claims and statements in the
books that I read. There was, though, a most significant fact that
emerged from the many different sources of information and this was
that one source tended to corroborate another and thus it was that,
for example, a book on Tibetan Lamaism would agree in certain concepts
with a book written by a medium and this in turn would be further confirmed by a book on the occult in general.

There began to emerge a pattern of confirmation that became like a
jigsaw puzzle of which I was gradually acquiring the pieces and they

were forming small sections that made sense. There were still many pieces of the puzzle missing and I was, in my mid-fifties, trying harder than ever to understand the real nature of life.

My own concept of God at that time was that of a kind of omniscient mental computer since the anthropomorphic concept of God held by many Christians was unacceptable to me. I had proved to myself that prayer can be very effective and I prayed ardently to God for some things that it had not previously been my privilege to enjoy. After many years, I received them.

Even then, I had very little understanding of the purely spiritual universe and I felt baffled. I had, I felt, come a long way and had increased my knowledge and understanding greatly but there was so much more to know and I knew there was.

The light finally began as a glimmer after I began to communicate directly with people in the spiritual world, or heaven, as they prefer to call it. In the space of about one year, that light grew in intensity until it was shining full in my eyes.

To my hundreds of questions I always received an answer. The most fundamental questions were disposed of first. There is a heaven but is there a hell? No, there is no actual hell in the religious sense. All people return to heaven whence they came, after death, but there are hell-like conditions in heaven, as there are on earth, created by the people themselves. They are reaping as they have sown. Do we live more than once? Yes, we all do. Is there a purpose in our earthly lives? Yes, there is. My questions nearly drove my Guides to distraction, if that were possible, but, to my delight, the answers not only made a great deal of sense but confirmed many of the conclusions that I had already reached during my many years of thought and study.

Gradually, I built up a complete picture of the nature of the spiritual universe. That which had earlier been incomprehensible to me now became clear as a result of the information given to me by my, by now, many spiritual advisors. I learned that, in appearance, heaven resembles the planet earth in that there are trees, flowers, rivers, lakes, mountains and buildings of all kinds. Heaven consists of seven planes and one realm above the seventh known as Sphere Eight.

A plane in heaven is a spiritual realm that reflects the state of mind of its occupants. The lowest plane, Plane One, or the astral plane, as it is also known, is divided into two regions, the lower astral and the upper astral. On the lower astral can be found the dregs of humanity living, as one would expect, in indescribable filth and squalor. Here are to be found the world's criminals, terrorists and tyrants. They are totally materialistic and show no interest at all in moral or ethical values. On the upper astral are spiritual beings who are not necessarily wicked but who have not progressed very far, spiritually, and who know little or nothing of the higher spiritual concepts.

After death, we return to heaven to a plane equivalent to our own spiritual height. Normally, incarnate people do not reach a height greater than that of Plane Four. After they die, they may continue to study until they graduate to Planes Five or Six subject to their kharmas having been completed and their having qualified, spiritually. The great majority of people on earth are of Plane One

11

height but not all of these are evil, merely unevolved spiritually. In general, the more highly spiritual a person is, the better his moral and ethical standards and the more he puts others before himself. Also, materialistic attitudes give way to the more important abstract qualities of life.

In the upper astral plane are those who were not necessarily criminal in their last lives but who were apathetic towards study and learning and who just drifted through life, taking it as it came.

Plane Two contains those who have finally broken some of the fetters of materialism and who take an interest in their own spiritual situations and are prepared to help themselves. Unfortunately, those who were very religious often cling to their false beliefs and practise as before, even to the extent of going to church. There are many churches on Planes One and Two whose adherents are so imbued with their respective religious teachings that, in spite of being shown the truth, they find themselves utterly unable to accept it, preferring the routine discipline of church ceremony.

As one advances to the higher planes, it becomes obvious that the higher spiritual beings show absolutely no interest in the beliefs of religions because, knowing the truth, they know them to be false. There are no churches on the higher planes.

The spiritual beings on Plane Three are much more pleasant, more knowledgeable and more capable than those below them and the same applies to those on each successive plane.

Planes Six and Seven are the equivalent of the Kingdom of Heaven as spoken of by religions. Once having reached Plane Five, one must have completed one's kharma which means that no further atonement is necessary and the Damoclean sword of reincarnation has been sheathed. Because spiritual beings are immortal, they live for ever on the highest planes in a state of heavenly bliss.

The highest attainable state in the universe is that of total responsibility combined with total ethics. This means that a High Spiritual Being is free to do anything that he or she wishes within the agreed-upon, self-imposed constraints necessary in a society where there are no negative emotions, no hatred, no greed, no jealousy, no envy, no attempts at self-aggrandisement, no pomposity and no unkind thoughts or acts. All behaviour is richly coloured by the emotion of love and a calm serenity radiates from High Spiritual Beings that is almost entirely lacking in spiritual beings below Plane Five.

The state of freedom combined with total responsibility constitutes the apogee of spiritual experience. The numinous notion that we are all one is not true at all. On the contrary, we are all individuals. Surely, it is an insult to the great men and women of our past to imply that they are one with the mass murderers and wicked tyrants who have been their contemporaries while incarnate. No! We are all different. We have all had widely different experiences. A musician's life cannot be compared with that of an aircraft pilot, for example.

Neither are we one with God. This is another religious concept that has no foundation in fact. God is an individual Being. We are not part of Him, nor He part of us. God is God. We are ourselves and this state cannot change. We cannot become one another, nor part of another. Our own minds are unique in the universe. God dwells on Plane Seven but He uses countless other spiritual beings to help Him in His great work.

He employs experts in all fields of human endeavour as consultants. Each plane has a Plane Leader and, at the time of writing, their names are as follows; Plane One, Samson; Plane Two, Mithra; Plane Three, Christian; Plane Four, Olivier; Plane Five, Christos; Plane Six, Tomas. God is supreme on Plane Seven and is, of course, superior to all spiritual beings on the planes below Him.

Above Plane Seven is a realm known as Sphere Eight. It is from here that the entire universe is governed by the Gardeners of the Earth. This fact is bound to be one of the most difficult to accept since people are told that God rules paramount in His Heaven.

Of course, the religions will, without exception, rise up against this information for it knocks the very foundations of their belief from under their feet. I stress the word belief because that is what religions are based upon, belief, NOT knowledge! The truth is very different from that which hundreds of millions of people on earth believe. It IS possible to know instead of believing.

The High Spiritual Beings who constitute the government, number only twelve. Four of these have never been incarnate but all of the others, except one, are characters of great prominence in the bible. Jesus Christ is a Gardener of the Earth but He prefers to work on Plane Seven. Jesus Christ acts as a kind of liaison officer between Sphere Eight and all the other planes.

Jesus Christ has an extremely bright aura and to visual psychics He appears to radiate an intense, lustrous luminescence. His robe sometimes scintillates with the glitter of a million diamond facets. On other occasions, I have marvelled at the wondrous beauty of His robe of pearl. It is as though it is made of mother-of-pearl in small,sequin-like segments. The pure whiteness is offset by a one-inch wide blue hem or border that is decorated with golden motifs.

The great and wonderful man's aura is blue and white, edged with yellow and gold. His hair is of shoulder length and it is golden yellow in colour. While incarnate, Christ's hair was black, however. Clear, calm, blue eyes illuminate the strong features of His face and He radiates an atmosphere of peace and love.

Throughout heaven, there are numerous buildings, more permanent than any on earth, that reflect the finest architecture and craftsmanship that have ever existed. Upon entering the Great Hall of Memories on Plane Four, one is struck by the differences between the spiritual world and earth. The rooms vary in size but all are illuminated by a spiritual light, the source of which cannot be detected. It is a beautiful, glowing brilliance that is never harsh.

Just inside the main entrance, one looks up into an enormous dome reminiscent of that of a cathedral but, of course, there is nothing pertaining to religion here. Passing through a passage with paintings on the walls, one enters an annexe containing statues and busts of famous people. Sculpted by the greatest artists of history who still practise their art in heaven, the likenesses are dramatic and lifelike and are, sometimes, in natural colour.

Occasionally, one comes upon a holographic painting. This technique is not known on earth but the effect is of a fully three-dimensional subject. Holograms are produced on earth by optical means but not in painted form.

Passing through another corridor, the vast library comes into view. The shelves of books appear to be endless and there is no shortage of subjects to study. Here may be found the great philosophical works by people like Plato and, of course, the complete works of William Shakespeare. Conspicuous by its absence is the bible which is responsible for creating such confusion in people's minds on earth. In its place is the Book of the Truth which defines the reality of the spiritual existence. This book is there for all to read but, incomprehensively, there are some who avoid learning the truth, preferring to adhere to fallacious doctrines. It is impossible to reach the higher planes, though, without accepting the truth so those who eschew the facts only limit their own progress.

Also in the Great Hall there are special rooms where reincarnation meetings are held. These are presided over by a High Spiritual Being and discussions take place concerning the next incarnation of a particular spiritual being. Suitable parents are selected and the person's kharma is outlined. Some spiritual beings reincarnate willingly, because they know that they cannot, otherwise, rise any further. Yet, others, fearing the retribution that they know is inescapable, are loath to reincarnate and only do so under great duress.

The Akashic Record is housed in the Great Hall. In it, a spiritual being can see him or herself as he or she was in all former lives. They can see why, for example, they had to suffer such hardship in their last incarnation, for they were atoning for misbehaviour in earlier lives.

Having been shown their past, the spiritual beings can see the purpose behind their kharmas and the need for further atonement. Those who have taken their own lives can see the futility of such an act because they know that they must reincarnate in order to try, once again, to come to terms with their kharma.

The Akashic Record hall resembles a cinema. There are seats and one sits facing a blank screen. Gradually, images appear and the person's past unfolds in all its aspects of drama, tragedy, work, war, suffering and happiness.

In the Great Hall are many committee rooms where spiritual beings sit to discuss topics of importance and to determine the conduct and spiritual advancement of people. Additionally, there are lecture rooms where they are taught the spiritual truths.

Outside the great building, one may saunter in the tranquil surroundings, admiring the fragrance of the beautifully-coloured flowers and gazing into the pools of crystal-clear water, some of which contain prettily-coloured fish. The verdure is greener and brighter than on earth and all colours are enhanced leaving the sensitive beholder imbued with a deep aesthetic feeling the like of which is rarely experienced on earth.

Probably, there are many on earth who, while accepting the fact of the after-life, find it difficult to understand what there is to do in heaven. The inscription R.I.P. on graves is ironic because no spiritual being rests in peace. By the time they have reached a state of mental peace, they are invariably bringing into play, for the benefit of others, their many talents. It is true to say that some, who never did a stroke of work while incarnate, find that they have to work after they die.

14

The widespread popular conception of people being laid to rest is, from the point of view of those in heaven, quite ridiculous. What, then, do we do? There are those, particularly women, who work with children who have returned to heaven, re-educating and rehabilitating them. Others teach medicine, music, art, finance, the great sciences and spiritual subjects. Those who do not lead by teaching, may study anything they wish to in the libraries or at the numerous lectures. Concerts are held where musicians perform the most amazing works of an ethereal quality, superior even to the greatest musical works on earth.

Plays are performed and William Shakespeare's work is still very popular and will always, deservedly, be so. Basically, any creative subject or activity practised on earth may be followed in heaven.

People of like experience meet to discuss their favourite topics and so the high-ranking naval men come together, the great politicians meet one another, the well-known composers of music are able to discuss their subjects and the famous philosophers congregate in order to commune with other deep thinkers.

In heaven, there is a meeting of the minds whereby people who were accustomed to exercising their intellects on earth may continue to do so. Like attracts like.

CHAPTER TWO

THE HEAVENLY LIFE

I am Tena writing through Alan Valiant about the life that I now enjoy in heaven. In my last incarnation, I was a Scotswoman and I died in 1780 in Scotland. As I had reached the spiritual height of Plane Two, I returned to that plane when I died.

Having received an excellent education at a finishing school as the daughter of a gentleman, I was used to diligent study which has stood me in good stead since, because, in heaven, there is so much to learn. It did not take me long to re-adapt myself to the spiritual life but I should like to explain to the reader what our world is like. After my departure from my physical body, I found that I still had a body, similar in shape with a head and limbs but flawless. In appearance, I had reverted to the age of nineteen. This is the spiritual body which retains the facial characteristics of the incarnate body but which rarely looks older than nineteen or twenty.

Our spiritual bodies feel as solid to us as our physical bodies did. Although we exist in an environment that is very similar to that of earth in many ways, there are some amazing differences. We do not seem to have internal body organs but we may eat and drink if we wish. Everything that we desire we produce by a thought process. For example, if I wish to eat a cake, I make a mental replica of one and it appears where I want it to in solid form. I can then eat it.

As I have no internal organs to process and dispose of the food as is the case with physical bodies, the cake, or whatever I eat or drink, diffuses into my body and is absorbed as a form of energy.

We cannot feel pain in our bodies but can experience a greater range of emotion than those on earth. Since our environment reflects our spiritual and mental state, we can recreate, for example, the home that we enjoyed on earth and, on Plane Six, my present plane, the beautiful cottage, in which I enjoyed a wonderful life with my dear husband and two children has been recreated for me by architects and builders who specialise in such work.

Everywhere on this plane are scenes of great beauty - flowers, trees, hills, valleys, rivers, seas and an eternal brilliance of an indescribably beautiful hue in the heavenly sky. There is no sun visible, however.

I communicate with my fellow spiritual beings either by speaking or by mental telepathy. If I wish to travel far, I merely think of where I wish to go and I am there. For short distances, I walk. Strictly speaking, space and time do not exist in heaven. There is an illusion of space but there is no time. Thus, it is possible to move instantaneously in both the spiritual and the physical universes.

As I have, finally, after numerous lives in physical bodies on planets, completed my kharma, I shall never have to reincarnate. I had to study and work hard to reach my present plane but the rewards are infinitely great and like nothing that one can experience on earth.

Some people wonder what we do here after we die, so I shall try to explain. As on earth, the amount of activity indulged in by spiritual beings is proportional to their ability to apply their intellect so that, on the lowest plane, one finds spiritual beings who waste every opportunity to improve themselves. They get up to mischief and annoy others and show no interest in self-advancement or helping others.

Although instructors are available and ready and willing to teach anyone who wants to be taught, many ignore them and fritter away their existence waiting only for the inevitable rebirth on earth to endure yet another life-time of atonement.

On Plane Two, the majority of spiritual beings show some interest in learning and in helping others. You may ask what there is to learn. Well, any subject that exists on earth may be studied in heaven. In addition, and very importantly, the spiritual existence itself must be studied and understood if the student is ever going to rise spiritually.

Experts in the arts descend from the higher planes in order to lecture and teach subjects such as music, painting, sculpture, engineering and so on. These sessions are of particular value to those about to be reincarnated with a definite career in mind. Thus, the would-be musician is born with a subconscious memory of his prior musical studies and, if his choice of parents and environment has been a wise one, he will succeed in pursuing a career as a musician.

On the other hand, those who have completed their kharmas and will not have to reincarnate are kept busy improving their own spiritual education and assisting others by passing on their experience.

Only by acquiring a deep understanding of the true nature of the spiritual universe and by shedding all negative characteristics and turning one's interest away from oneself in order to help others can a spiritual being rise to the higher planes. Self-interest is not a characteristic of High Spiritual Beings but a genuine desire to help others, is.

Numerous lady instructors give valuable advice on how to bring up a family to those about to reincarnate as females.

We cannot work indefinitely without rest or relaxation and we may retire to our homes to sleep or we can take advantage of the numerous wonderful social occasions in heaven. For example, there are orchestral concerts of all kinds of music including Western and Eastern classical music. Those who enjoy jazz or other, lighter forms of music may either play in a band or simply listen to the musicians enjoying themselves.

The reader will, by now, have realised that life in heaven is very similar to that on earth in many respects. The most remarkable differences are obvious on the higher planes where there is an intense spiritual light and where the feeling is one of buoyancy and ebullience.

Any dweller on a high plane is likely to dislike descending to a lower one, particularly Plane One, unless to serve others, because to travel from Plane Six to Plane One may be compared with leaving the earth's surface in brilliant sunshine and descending in a mine shaft to a region of almost total darkness.

I, Tena, am a very privileged spiritual being because I have been granted permission by God to remain twenty-four hours a day with an incarnate being. Except for the purposes of communication, spiritual beings are not normally permitted to remain on earth because it retards their spiritual progress and can confuse their incarnate associates.

As Alan Valiant and I are soul-mates and because he works very hard
on behalf of the spiritual world in the interests of spreading the
truth, I am with him continuously and shall be for ever. I am able to
help him with his domestic chores and also his spiritual work as I am
doing at this moment. Because I am always at his side, Alan
communicates with me frequently. While he is working, unless I am able
to help, I remain silent but if he needs advice on his shopping, for
example, then he consults me.

We are completely in tune with one another's thoughts and
predilections. Because I am able to read his mind, there is absolutely
nothing that Alan can think, do or say without my knowledge. This
situation would horrify many people but, because he understands that
not only I but many other High Spiritual Beings are observing him
continuously also, Alan accepts the situation and is grateful in the
knowledge that he is considered important enough to warrant such close
attention from people in the highest realms of heaven.

During some nights, another High Spiritual Being, a former Tibetan
Lama, and I take Alan from his body while he sleeps and we all travel
in the astral. Astral travellers are not usually allowed to go higher
than Plane Four unless they are invited by a High Spiritual Being, but
Alan and I have been taken as high as Plane Seven.

Sometimes we travel to a place in the physical universe such as
Yolland Allicay, known as the reward planet. Here, the inhabitants no
longer make war, there is no strife and they have a well-regulated
society run on the highest ethical standards. They do not need keys
because there are no criminals. Outwardly, the planet closely
resembles many parts of earth. There are lakes, rivers, seas and
transportation systems very similar to those on earth.

The Allicayans work for their livings but are content and never
clamour for more or go on strike. Family life is calm, suicide is
unknown, murder is non-existent and education for all is as good as it
is possible to be. Yolland Allicay represents the standard of
existence that IS achievable on earth but which, at the present rate
of retrogression, is not likely to be seen for at least a millennium.
Even the planet of Allicay is, itself, benign. There are no extremes
of weather and no earthquakes or famines. The planet lies in a
different galaxy from that of earth but, as I have said, distance is
of no significance to a spiritual being in the spiritual world. Alan
and I have sat on a mountain top on Allicay and admired the scenery
and we have watched the inhabitants playing games, including a variety
of football.

Spiritual beings are sometimes reincarnated to Yolland Allicay in
order to complete some minor atonement in the most favourable
conditions.

On the higher planes, all perceptics are prodigiously enhanced, in
comparison with those of the incarnate being. For example, colours
appear richer, purer and more beautiful and the plants and flowers
seem to irradiate a kind of love to the beholder. It is as though they
are saying, "I am beautiful, thank you for admiring me." There are
hues in heaven the like of which do not exist on earth, particularly
in the sky which is often changing colour in a fascinating way. It may
be compared with a thousand rainbows intertwining, with blendings of
colour weaving myriad patterns.

Music and sound take on an incredible sonorescent character and are frequently omniphonic, seeming to emanate from everywhere simultaneously. Lighting in the public buildings is diffused, its source seldom discernible. Usually, the intensity varies almost imperceptibly and in such a way as to contribute to the emotional impact of the particular subject of interest.

The great public buildings in heaven reflect the architectural skill of the most accomplished architects and artisans of the past. All styles and periods are represented and, standing beside a Roman style public building with its round and fluted stone columns , there may be an edifice in the oriental style with beautifully decorated pagodas.

Within the buildings may be found the greatest works of man, perpetuated for all to see. Paintings of every epoch and of any conceivable subject adorn the walls in some of the rooms. In others, giant, lifelike murals dominate the environment. Chariots pulled by panting horses appear to leap from the wall, leviathians of the sea sail past in majestic splendour, the spray catching the sunlight and reflecting a multitude of star-like points of light.

In the Hall of Statues, there are the finest examples of the sculptor's art dating from the earliest times of man. Some busts are of marble, others of terra-cotta, while the realism of many is uplifted by the application of natural colour. The people represented in statuary include, of course, the greatest in history but, in addition, there are many fine sculptures of people who did not become famous in life. Owing to their significant contributions to the benefit of others during their lifetimes on earth, they are commemorated by the sculptors who may refer to the spiritual being's akashic record in order to achieve authenticity in every detail.

The Hall of Machinery contains a fascinating collection of machines of every kind dating from millions of years ago, many of which were in use on other inhabited planets. All may be seen working and there are engineers on hand to explain them to the visitors. In the field of speed records, there is an entire hall devoted to the machines and the men and women who drove them or flew them. The aircraft section, as may be imagined, is vast. It comprises a complete history of man's modern and most recent conquest of the air including every kind of flying machine.

Stated briefly, the entire historical panorama of man's endeavours in the physical universe is displayed for the enjoyment, wonderment and inspiration of all spiritual beings. Earth's museums, excellent though many are, cannot begin to approach these superb displays of human achievement over millions of years throughout the entire universe.

A vast natural history hall exhibits animal, bird, insect and fish forms that have existed since Creation. To those sufficiently interested, any of the creatures may be studied as they were in their own time by reference to the Akashic Record. Utter realism is portrayed by the animal forms and one is left stunned by their sheer beauty, complexity and ability.

To those who believe that death is the end, I wish to say, "Look forward to your return to heaven but be certain your conscience is clear." If you can honestly say to yourself, "Well, I have had a difficult life but I have really tried to do my best," then you have little to fear because you will, most likely, have risen at least one more rung on the ladder of spirituality. The main reason that many fear death is that the inner, small voice of their spiritual conscience is reminding them of their transgressions in earlier lives. They know, subconsciously, why they were born and guilt is the father of fear.

It is not others that you need to fear, nor any thought of punishment by God because, whatever happens to you after you die, you must have deserved it. If, on the other hand, you have led a dissipated, wayward, selfish life, then you can be secure in the knowledge that further incarnations await you so that you will have opportunities to eliminate the negative characteristics of your personality. However you may have behaved in your present life, one inescapable fact supersedes all others; you will receive your just desserts.

CHAPTER THREE

HEREDITY

Written by Donald Campbell through the Author.

While a great deal is known today about genetics and heredity , there still appears to be much confusion as to which human characteristics are capable of being inherited and which are not. In the first place, there are two lines of inheritance, the genetic line and the spiritual line.

The human genetic line has continued, of course, unbroken since the reproduction of the species began, otherwise they would have died out. Through the normal processes of procreation, the human species has flourished for millions of years and there are many dominant characteristics of heredity that must be perfectly obvious to anyone, such as skin colour, high cheekbones, fuzzy hair, straight hair and so on.

Further, in accordance with the laws discovered by Mendel, a monk who lived in the nineteenth century, eye and hair colouring and physical features such as body height and shape of nose are fairly predictable when certain characteristics of the parents are known. Two blond-haired parents are highly likely to produce a child with blond hair unless a recessive trait is carried by the genes of one or both which may produce a dark-haired child. This atavistic characteristic occurs infrequently as the genes producing it may lie dormant for many generations.

All major physical characteristics are hereditary but these are modified, in the majority of cases, by the influence of the spiritual being upon his physical body. Throughout successive incarnations there is a recognisable similarity of the features regardless of whether one was male or female. This partly explains why children never grow up to look exactly like their parents. The basic features of the spiritual being, perfect as they are in the spiritual world, are imprinted upon the genetic structure of the physical body.

The inheritance of diseases is another subject of much controversy. Physical diseases may be passed on by contagion as with congenital syphilis, for example, but those that "run in families" occur because it is the kharma of those family members to suffer them. Group kharma is quite common, resulting in whole families reincarnating many times often with an interchanged relationship such as the parent of a child in one life becoming the child of that same being in a later life. In order to resolve their individual kharmas, they must atone collective-ly.

Many suspected cases of inherited illness are merely the result of a bad example having been set by one or both parents and copied by the son or daughter. Living a life of excess will, almost invariably, produce symptoms of physical disorder, eventually, and so the gourmand becomes obese, the regular beer drinker finds his equator expanding to undesirable proportions, the inveterate spirits drinker may suffer disorders such as cirrhosis of the liver and the habitual smoker may suffer bronchitis and more serious lung complaints. It can be said that all of these maladies have been self-induced. It is wrong to

21

ascribe them to heredity.

The second line of inheritance, although not second in importance, is the spiritual one. As spiritual beings, we have long existed in some form or other, either discarnate or incarnate and, today, we have inherited from our own past lives, combined with our learning between lives in heaven, a vast amount of experience of all kinds. We have occupied many physical bodies but our basic identity that is our own mind cannot be terminated nor obliterated.

A man who sent Christians to the lions in the Roman arena two thousand years ago may be a present-day bank clerk suffering from cancer. The much-acclaimed military hero of the barbarian age may be a woman slaving in a deprived community today. Between those lives, these individuals may have lived numerous others, depending on their kharmic state. They are, though, the same beings throughout, although their behaviour may be different from life to life as they progress spiritually.

Mental ability is NOT inherited from one's parents. It may often appear to be so but consider the spiritual being in heaven who has acquired a good academic standard in a past life and who, knowing he must reincarnate in order to atone, carefully chooses his parents. He will endeavour to choose intellectual parents who will realise the great value of a good education and therefore he will be given the best possible environment in which to develop his scholastic talents.

In this way, academic ability frequently runs in families but there are many exceptions. It may happen that an intellectually-minded person has to reincarnate into a poor and badly educated family for kharmic reasons. There are numerous examples of people rising to great heights from humble beginnings but neither their mental ability nor their intellect is inherited from their parents. These qualities are acquired over a very long period of time and after a number of incarnations and are the result of experiences, observations, goals achieved and habits of study adopted.

If the kharmic drive is sufficiently strong, the person will overcome all problems such as poverty, dialect and class in order to complete the kharma that he returned to earth to fulfil.

From the foregoing, it is obvious that a child owes only its physical existence to its parents. They, through the normal process of procreation, created the vehicle for the spiritual being that will inhabit it until it ceases to function at death. The being that is the inhabitant of the child's body has previously existed and is an individual entity entirely separate from its parents.

It follows that parents cannot own their children because their progeny are individual beings in their own right. They come *through* their parents but are not *of* them. The young child may have died of old age in his previous life and could have acquired a wealth of knowledge and ability. The concept of a child as an empty vessel waiting to be filled with experience is not a true one. He is, rather, a partly-filled vessel waiting to be topped up. The child may have had vastly more total experience than either parent and this will usually soon make itself known. Every human life with which a parent or parents are entrusted is sacred and any parental failure to provide the physical and spiritual comforts essential to the natural development of their offspring is bound to invite negative kharma provided it is the result of negligence or apathy and not caused by the restrictions of the environment.

As has been explained, one cannot own one's children but, nevertheless, it is the obligation of the parents to foster the needs of their youngsters until they are able to cope alone with the problems of living.

It is the parents' responsibility to guide the child but never to force him or her to follow a particular course of action or a certain profession. Guidance is the keynote. The decision should always rest with the child. Admittedly, some children suffer from inertia, the same as many adults do, and these may need a nudge or two in order to stimulate them into appropriate action, but excessive coercion, tantamount to suppression, must be avoided at all costs. This particularly applies to the imparting of religious knowledge to children. Those youngsters who are unfortunate enough to be born of deeply religious parents have an additional hazard to face compared with others more favourably placed.

From birth, they will be indoctrinated and drilled in religious jargon and practices until their behaviour, in many cases, will become automatic and without consideration or thought. The fortunate ones, able to shine the light of their intelligence into the darkness of erroneous teachings may, with considerable difficulty, and often family embarrassment, eventually escape to find that they are able to view the objects of religious attention from an independent, unaberrated viewpoint. The numinous idiosyncracies of parents are transmitted to their children, many of whom, utterly indoctrinated, perpetuate the fallacies and ensure that through their own descendants, ignorance of the truth will prevail.

In summary, there are two lines of heredity, the phylogenetic line, in which one is dependent upon parents for passing on the various characteristics that every human body possesses and the spiritual line in which behaviour, ability and understanding are dependent upon one's total experience throughout many lives on planets combined with spiritual height as indicated by one's plane number.

23

CHAPTER FOUR

SIN

In its most basic form, Christianity is succinctly expressed by its followers as, "sinners go to hell and those who have been "saved" shall have eternal life." Firstly, there is no hell to which sinners are sent by God. The earth is the only punishment planet in the universe and life on earth in physical bodies is hell. Any hell-like situation in which a spiritual being finds himself after death is entirely the result of his own attitudes and behaviour and there are regions of the lower astral plane that *are* hell-like. The environment there merely reflects the standards of its inhabitants.

Secondly, no other person, incarnate or discarnate, can save YOU from the consequences of your expressed views and your actions, not even Jesus Christ or God can do that. If you commit a sin, you MUST atone for it if you are ever to rise spiritually. Let us, now, examine what exactly constitutes a sin and what does not, for each sect has its own list of sins.

MURDER

This is the worst sin because the taking of another's life can thwart the kharma carefully planned by God for the victim. However, a person who is murdered and was not intended to die in such a way is compensated in heaven or in a subsequent incarnation for having had his kharma interrupted through no fault of his own. The murderer automatically ensures that he, himself, will be reincarnated in order to atone for his crime. It does not always happen that the punishment fits the crime and a murderer may or may not die in a subsequent life by the hand of another but it is certain that his atonement through suffering will be at least equal to that which he caused his victim. Diseases such as cancer in its various forms are frequently imposed as atonement for serious crimes committed in former lives.

The only exceptional cases in which atonement will not be implemented are those where life is taken purely accidentally as opposed to negligently, and in self-defence.

A soldier, forced to fight, does not have to atone for every member of the enemy that he kills or wounds but, if he deliberately tortures or kills prisoners of war,then he will atone and very heavily. Drivers who kill people while drunk will atone. A responsible driver confronted by a situation where, for example, a child dashes out in front of his car and is killed, will not have to atone.

The terrorist, far from furthering what he firmly believes is his own and justifiable good cause, has a terrible effect upon his own kharma. The lower astral plane contains thousands of "dead" terrorists who are reaping the frightful effects of their horrific anti-social activities while incarnate. They will all, without exception, return to earth, many of them to become victims of their own violent organisations, thereby experiencing the fear and suffering that they have caused others.

SUICIDE

Taking one's own life is, without any doubt, the most stupid act that a person can commit. It is, primarily, a crime against oneself but most suicides cause anguish to their relatives and friends and are then harming others. Suicides automatically ensure a further incarnation in order to confront the same kinds of problem that over-whelmed them to the point of self-destruction.We are on earth to learn how to cope with life's situations but each person has at least one major basic behaviour characteristic with which he must learn to come to terms.

The person who abused the privilege of riches will have to learn how to handle money; the arrogant must learn humility; the violent must learn gentleness; the sexually depraved must learn to use sex as it should be used, to the mutual benefit of its participants; the homosexual must readjust to a heterosexual existence; the thief must learn to respect the property of others; the megalomaniac must learn to use positions of power with a humble understanding of the problems of others; the alcoholic and the drug-taker must learn that excess in all things leads to self-destruction and that they, alone, can control their actions for they have free will; the religious zealot must learn that high spirituality cannot be reached through the tenets and practices of any religion.

No matter what the pressures may be upon a person, suicide invokes severe atonement. As usual, the human mind, corrupted as it is from birth by the misunderstandings and false teachings of parents, teachers and associates, is unable to make a rational assessment of a given situation. This leads the potential suicide to believe that he is "ending it all". Instead, he is starting again! It cannot be stressed too strongly that suicide is a futile act bound to involve the person in similar unpleasant situations in a future life or lives.

No one is ever destined to die by taking his own life and those who do so merely extend the time that they will take to reach the point of no return in heaven which is Plane Five. The only way to rise spirit-ually, when involved in situations that reduce one to a state of despair, is to fight back. Help may usually be obtained from someone and a person in such a state is in need of help. Once having brought oneself from the bitter trough of desperate despair back up to a state of lively interest in life, the experience becomes of value to the extent that it will have been the crucible in which the flame of cour-age has been kindled.

SEX

Rape is a very serious sin that attracts a heavy penalty as does any other sexual act where force, violence or threats of violence are employed to achieve gratification.

The sexual perversion of children is a sin. Whereas prostitution as such, is not a sin where the woman practises it willingly, those who force girls into prostitution who, otherwise would have chosen a virt-uous career, are inviting kharmic retribution.

Sex with a partner other than one's spouse is not a sin, although adultery is still punishable by death in Islamic law, for example. Society, however, imposes restrictions upon such associations and these are desirable in a well-balanced community. When the sexual esc-apades of any person become merely orientated towards physical gratification, to the total exclusion of love, or they occupy the majority of one's interest and a state of profligacy exists, then the sin is against oneself. This means that, in a subsequent life, one will have to learn to come to terms with the sexual urge and use it in a reasonable manner and with a balanced outlook.

Between consenting adults, there is no sexual act that can be considered sinful. This applies to homosexuals and lesbians as well because these relationships are often founded upon a love basis. The law in Europe in the past, based as it was upon the churches' view of sin, has been terribly wrongly applied. Until comparatively recently, men could be hanged for homosexual acts. Why this did not apply to lesbians is difficult to understand but it stems mainly from the puritanical preachings of Christians wherein anything connected with sex was regarded as dirty.

Such was, and still is, in many cases, the state of mental aberration of those whose moral standards and state of spiritual awareness were dictated to them by priests. To sum up, sex between people in love is not a sin and may be practised whenever the partners feel mutually inclined to re-affirm the consummation of their love. To assert, as some people do, that sex should only be indulged in for procreation purposes, is entirely missing the point. A true and lasting love relationship demands both mental and physical compatibility and the frequent union of the partners in confirmation of their true feelings for each other.

While incarnate, sex serves the dual purpose of procreation and the satisfaction of the irresistible sexual urge. In heaven, exactly the same act performed between male and female spiritual beings serves to seal the love knot, since procreation of spiritual beings by spiritual beings is impossible. Love between the sexes in heaven is consummated in exactly the same way as on earth. The spiritual bodies, that feel solid to spiritual beings, are perfectly-formed counterparts of their former physical bodies and even the highest spiritual beings in heaven enjoy sexual relationships. The often-quoted notion that one discards an interest in sex as one rises spiritually is not valid.

Sexual self-gratification is not a sin and, in the absence of a natural heterosexual relationship, is even desirable since repression of one's sexual urge on imagined moral grounds inevitably results in a psychological conflict that can render a person neurotic, to say the least. Self-relief is society's sexual safety valve. Neither is it sinful to fantasize a sexual relationship with a member of the opposite sex who attracts one but who may be unattainable. Without such interest in the act of love, the whole purpose of it would be defeated so no person need feel guilty about imagining a sexual encounter. In summary, thinking about sex is not sinful.

One's whole approach to sex should be, as with everything else in life, one of complete responsibility and a total readiness to accept the consequences of one's own actions.

ANIMALS

Domestic animals depend upon man for their welfare and existence so the person who decides to look after an animal takes upon himself full responsibility for ensuring that it receives enough food of the right kind, is protected from attacks by other animals and humans and is treated with kindness and understanding. Animals have feelings and are able to communicate with other animals and humans telepathically but, unfortunately, they are regarded as "dumb" because they cannot speak. It is true that they cannot speak in words but they can convey their thoughts by their actions in addition to projecting telepathic concepts.

The owner of animals, whether a farmer or a pet keeper, who maltreats his animals commits a sin or crime.   Beating or starving animals invokes kharmic retribution. Raising animals for food and then slaughtering them is not a sin provided the killing is quickly and humanely carried out.   It is not a sin to eat meat of any kind except that human flesh may be eaten only in emergency and after natural or accidental death in order to save other lives.

Further,   the hunting and killing of animals that are not required for food or clothing is a sin but hunting in order to survive is a legitimate act that does not attract atonement unless cruelty is involved. Hunting big game merely for prestige is a crime and the wilful destruction of elephants and tigers, for example, to use the tusks and skins as trophies, is bound to attract an unpleasant kharma. Blood sports are crimes against the animal kingdom.

GAMBLING

Gambling is not a sin but if a man habitually gambles away his income thereby causing hardship to his family, then that is sinful. If someone has money to spare and gambles without causing anyone else harm, no crime is committed. If the gambler renders himself destitute, then the sin is against himself.

FINANCIAL CRIMES

Theft of money, no matter how it is carried out, embezzlement, falsification of documents or interference with computers to gain a pecuniary advantage and forging cheques or other forms involving money are all crimes and will be atoned for. Taking money under false pretences such as charging a customer for work that has not been carried out is also a crime. Briefly, any act that deprives a person, organisation or government of money that rightly belongs to them is a sin.

WILFUL DESTRUCTION

Vandalism, for some inexplicable reason, is seldom punished by law, in Britain at least, although it costs the country millions of pounds every year. Not only is it an offence in law but it is also a sin and the wreckers and destroyers pay heavily for their fun later in their existence.

ABORTION

The deliberate termination of the life of an embryo, unless to save the mother from death, constitutes a sin.   It is no less a crime than infanticide.   The embryo is a human entity and has been incarnated by God. The spiritual being may be attached by the silver cord to the embryo at any time from conception to the quickening, about four months.   Destruction of the unborn foetus is a sin against God and thwarts His planned destiny for the unborn child. Women who use abortion instead of contraceptive methods of avoiding an unwanted

27

child are building up bad kharma and those members of the medical profession who readily agree to terminate pregnancies for reward and without just cause are inevitably going to have to atone for their crimes.

CONTRACEPTION

Contrary to Roman Catholic dogma, the use of artificial means of contraception is not a sin but is highly desirable where the alternatives are unwanted children or large families that cannot be properly fed or educated. However, vasectomy and removal of the womb or ovaries merely to avoid further conceptions are highly undesirable because they may alter the kharma of the people concerned. A man may be intended to raise three children but if, after one or two, he is vasectomised, he will have altered his kharma.

The same reasoning applies to a woman who is sterilised. Man has free will to control the number of offspring that he fathers and this legitimises artificial means since no method is one hundred percent reliable and his kharma will usually be achieved.

GENERAL

According to many religions, failure to pay alms to the church or to conform with the religious calendar regarding fasting are sins. These are merely two of the numerous artifices devised by the churches to suppress and hold their congregations. The sins are committed by the churches in enforcing such restrictions upon their followers. Of course, many people happily conform with such disciplines because they believe that they are the way to salvation.

To deprive oneself of food, like any other penance whether self-imposed or enforced from without, is a purposeless, masochistic pursuit and cannot possibly enhance one's standing before God or raise one spiritually. Prohibited foods and beverages feature prominently among the lists of religious "sins" but the truth of the matter is that there is *no* food or drink the consumption of which is sinful. Extremists who limit their liquid intake to water are labouring under considerable misapprehension engendered, no doubt, by the ancient idea that asceticism is an essential ingredient in the formula to be followed to ensure salvation.

You may eat or drink anything you wish. The only considerations are those of health and responsibility. Never eat or drink to excess and consume only that which you consider is good and necessary for your health.

The consumption of alcohol is not a sin but any crime committed while under its influence is a sin and there can be no question that the responsibility of the individual for his behaviour is in no way diminished while he is inebriated.

Blackmail, extortion, kidnap, demanding ransom and bearing false witness are but a few of the well-known overt acts against others. All of these and any similar act against another person constitute sins and will be atoned for.

The cause in which a crime is committed is irrelevant. A crime is a sin. It is the *intention* behind the act that determines guilt.

CHAPTER FIVE

SPIRITUAL PSYCHIATRY

Written by Professor Doctor Carl Jung through the Author.

Any form of applied psychiatry that fails to include a comprehensive understanding of man as a spiritual being is a false psychiatry. The word is derived from the Greek "psyche", the personification of the soul, and "iatros", a physician. The modern definition of the psyche is "soul, spirit, mind". A practitioner of psychiatry should, by definition, be primarily concerned with the spiritual welfare of his patients so why is it that the psychiatry of today is almost entirely aligned along the materialistic, physical approach?

The answer lies in the fact that psychiatrists, in general, tend to eschew any reference to the soul because that to them has religious connotations and, thinking themselves to be entirely practical, objective and down to earth practitioners of an established profession they frequently adhere to the chemical medicine techniques that they inherited from their medical fraternity.

The human being is regarded by the psychiatric establishment as a physical body entirely controlled by a brain. This concept is totally false and is responsible for great suffering endured by mental patients in the name of mental health.

Because of this limitation on the understanding of the true nature of man, psychiatry is almost entirely misapplied. Physical means are employed in a usually vain attempt to alleviate a mental disorder. A tiny minority of cases of abnormal behaviour have a physical cause. In nearly all of these, the origin of the aberration will be found in brain damage, however caused, or in the introduction of noxious substances to the body in whatever form.

When the psychiatric profession is prepared to jettison its Freudian concepts in favour of purely spiritual ones, great advances will be made in the mental welfare establishments. The current overcrowding in mental hospitals is a direct indictment against contemporary methods. The success rate in the profession is extremely low and this is not surprising.

When one considers that, in the twentieth century, doctors and psychiatrists are involved in applying electric currents to people's brains often resulting in cellular brain damage, in order to attempt to ameliorate some purely emotional condition, then the true horror of the present approach may be discerned. The attitude seems to be, "If the treatment produces a change then it must be working." How naive an approach this is! Electro-convulsive "therapy", along with many other techniques, is tantamount to a mediaeval style of torture that does nothing but harm to the trusting victim.

Criticism of psychiatry can be justified on more than one ground. Firstly, many of the modern methods are immoral and, secondly, they achieve few positive results. Thirdly, they are almost entirely based upon the completely false assumption that man is only body and brain.

Has any doctor or psychiatrist ever discovered the location of the spirit, mind or soul? No! Yet they refer to the mind which they erroneously believe to be the brain.

Let us, now, revert to the very basic *facts* of existence that are
unacceptable to western societies and, in particular, to most
psychiatrists. In the first place, man is a spiritual being and as
such is immortal. He dwells for the length of a lifetime in a body
composed of meat. *Before* our births, we already existed. During our
earthly lives, we exist and, after the death of our bodies, we continue to exist.

What is it then that continues to exist, since the physical body
can be seen to have decayed along with its brain? It is the mind and
spirit that constitute a spiritual being that persist after the
corporeal remains have been disposed of. There follows a definition of
the mind that I wrote through the author on 15th September, 1979.

CARL JUNG'S DEFINITION OF THE MIND

1   The mind is the spiritual repository of memory.
2   The mind is the centre of intelligence of the spiritual entity.
3   The mind is the motivator.
4   The mind is the sensory centre.
5   The mind is the centre of emotion.
6   The mind is capable of evaluating and of calculating mathemat-
    ically.
7   Postulates created by the mind determine action.
8   The mind is non-physical.
9   The contents of the human mind determine spiritual status.
10 The mind is the centre of will.
11 The state of the mind influences the physical condition of the
    body.
12 The mind is capable of being influenced by external physical
    factors.
13 The mind may be influenced by other minds.
14 The mind survives the death of the body.
15 While incarnate, memories of previous lives are suppressed but
    remain, usually inaccessably, in the subconscious part of the
    mind.
16 It is the content of the subconscious mind that is responsible
    for the great majority of psychiatric disorders.
17 The condition of every human being, whether incarnate or
    discarnate, is the direct end result of his or her experiences,
    abilities, mental processes and attitudes acquired and
    accumulated during his or her total existence of many
    incarnations and immeasurable periods of earth time in heaven.

Any biological experiments that appear to indicate that memories
are being stored in living cells are being misinterpreted. Because
such experiments are carried out by psychiatrists or psychologists,
the results and findings are interpreted only through materialist-
ically prejudiced eyes. The concept of a spiritual mind is usually
beyond the practitioner's ability to grasp, therefore he firmly
believes that the seat of memory, senses and emotions is in the brain.
It is not! The brain is a vital organ and among its functions are the
servo-control of the locomotor muscles in the body, the control of the
endocrine secretions, the maintenance of equilibrium of the oxygen and

carbon dioxide content of the blood and the conversion of neurological signals into a computerised form of information, e.g.visual, auditory, tactile, olfactory and gustatory.   The brain is also responsible for the control of the routine functions of the body such as metabolism, cell regeneration, the heartbeat, thermostatic control and the provision of suitable physical conditions to enable a wound, for example, to be healed but, and it is a very big but, we sense nothing with the brain, only with the mind and it is the mind, linked to the brain for the duration of incarnate life, that monitors the signals in the brain.

By these means the body is influenced for good or bad by the mental state of the person.   Animals are no different from humans in their basic form, for mind is always present in every living animate form no matter whether it be an amoeba or an advanced primate.

Psycho-analysis, when properly carried out, can be very effective and is usually only limited in its therapeutic effect by the measure of the practitioner's understanding of the true nature of his patient.

As stated in article seventeen of my previously given definition of the mind, we are the end result of our experiences, abilities, mental processes and attitudes acquired and accumulated during our total existence of many incarnations. Thus, it can be seen that what we did or what happened to us in earlier lives can affect us in the present.

People are reincarnated in order to atone and to learn to rid themselves of undesirable attitudes,   so the person who had a violent temper in his last life and who has been reincarnated in order to learn to control it,   may continue to exhibit a bad temper thereby causing distress to his family and others.

Because his memory of why he is incarnate is deep in his subconscious mind and because he has been given free will,   the person casts around for the probable reason for his behaviour.   Unable to rationalise his condition, he may approach a psychiatrist who will usually, in the first instance, prescribe tranquillisers. These, while exerting a containing effect upon the patient, can never help either him or the psychiatrist to remove the basic cause of the hot temper or the violent actions that follow the breakdown of emotional control.

If psycho-analysis is applied by a person, not necessarily a train- ed physician and psychiatrist, but one who really understands that people have lived before, then there is a strong possibility that the original cause of the present-time aberration will be discovered.

Once the patient has confronted his previous-life behaviour, for which he is atoning now,   and has accepted responsibility for his own actions, the symptoms will recede and finally vanish.

Typical cases of previous life causation of present life traumas are those of acrophobia, fear of heights; agoraphobia, fear of open spaces and claustrophobia, fear of confined spaces.   No amount of physical treatment to a victim of one of these phobias can ever produce a cure.

Psycho-surgery, another false and entirely destructive weapon in the hands of psychiatrists, produces only disastrous effects upon the victim and, if the original aberration appears to have disappeared after such surgery, it will be only because a far worse condition has been exchanged for it in the form of dissociation and apathy.

As an example, here is an actual case history. Mary Jukes, a pseudonym, has an irrational fear of heights. Examination of her akashic record showed that, in the year 1066, she lived in Sutone, now known as Sutton, a district of Plymouth in the county of Devon, England and was married with two children. She loved her children but hated her husband on account of his libidinous sexual behaviour towards her.

One day, the family were out walking along the cliffs near the town when Mary deliberately pushed her husband over the edge and killed him. Although she has had further incarnations since that one, the trauma associated with the murder of her husband has remained with her to this day. Whenever Mary sees a high cliff or has to go near a high point on a building, she feels ill and uncomfortable. This is the subconscious memory being reawakened and turning on some of the emotion that she experienced after her original act of violence.

Until psychiatrists stop regarding people as "once only" entities and learn that they have all lived in physical bodies before, little progress is likely to be made. It is all very well, as an exercise, to categorise mental maladies and to give them fancy names but the name does not matter. It is the true nature of the illness and its root cause that are of major importance.

As the causes of the majority of mental disorders are far from obvious and since they are invariably different for each patient, although the symptoms may be similar, no fixed approach may be laid down in a text book that prescribes drugs, for example.

Numerous cases on the books of psychiatrists are currently victims of undesirable attentions from people discarnate. There are laws in heaven that forbid interference, as opposed to assistance, by spiritual beings with people on earth. As on earth, however, laws are broken in heaven and this is one of them. Some low spiritual beings, unscrupulous, hateful, spiteful, jealous or just plain mischievous, do deliberately try to harm incarnate beings. They may create their mental chaos by many means but the easiest, when the incarnate being is low in spirits, is that of telepathically projecting images into the victim's mind. Because the originator's mind is aberrated, the pictures so projected frequently resemble hallucinatory images.

The recipient of the mental images knows that he did not originate them and begins to question his sanity. In extreme cases, such people are classified as schizophrenes. There are two possible remedies for this condition. The first is for the victim to resist strongly any thought or image that he knows he did not originate and to fight back. The second and permanent cure is to remove the offending low spiritual being from the vicinity of the victim. This is tantamount to exorcism but traditional methods of doing this are quite unnecessary. When a low spiritual being is confronted by a High Spiritual Being, either discarnate or incarnate, he will always give way. He may bluster and rave but a calm, higher entity is more than a match for a low entity.

This means that an understanding and firmly determined person on earth can locate the perpetrator of the victim's mental condition, confront him and, after explaining that such behaviour will eventually rebound onto himself, order him to leave.

Such an act requires a very confident and understanding psychic. Visual psychics can see the malefactor. When communication with the spiritual world is more generally practised on a high level of understanding, conversations between the two domains will become commonplace and psychiatry will either have to change its approach radically or give way to the spiritually enlightened who really understand the nature of man and his spiritual and mental problems.

From birth until death, many unfortunate people suffer needlessly on account of the false information that they are given by parents, teachers and associates. They suffer while young because parents do not realise that their children have almost certainly been incarnate in human form before. The new-born babe, crying in its cot, may have been an old man of much wisdom in its previous life on earth, yet it is looked upon as being an entirely original creation.

As the child develops talents, it may be observed that it "has a good brain". The brain is a physical entity constructed of millions of cells but it *is* matter and matter cannot create anything. There is no life in matter and, above all, there is no intelligence in matter.

Intelligence is a spiritual faculty that one never loses. There are beings of the lowest and the highest intelligences in heaven. Directly after death, one is no less and no more intelligent than one was before it.

Those who have acquired the habit of study while on earth, have few problems in learning after they return to heaven. It must be thoroughly understood that learning continues in heaven but, as on earth, those who are apathetic towards study, or who cannot be bothered to strain their minds, make no progress.

You are on earth for two basic reasons, to atone for past crimes and to learn vital lessons. If you meander haphazardly through life, avoiding using your mind constructively whenever possible and pursuing a hedonistic existence, then you will have advanced but little by the time you pass on and will certainly, in due course, reincarnate yet again in order to make up for your wasted time.

One often hears someone say, "We are here to enjoy ourselves". Certainly, enjoyment is a desirable and legitimate experience when it is in balance with all other experiences but it is not the chief reason for our existence.

The greatest pleasure is to be obtained from constructive work and helping others but watching a stage or film presentation may bring pleasure. It is the superficial and artificial pleasures that some people pursue daily that lead nowhere. Such activities as compulsive gambling, drinking and smoking may give some an ephemeral sense of joy but it is a shallow joy and, all too frequently, the kind that can turn to sorrow and even tragedy. The gambler may become a bankrupt, the drinker may become an alcoholic and the smoker may die of bronchitis or lung cancer.

The activities that bring the greatest pleasure are usually those from which others benefit. Creative work such as house building or decorating, music, art in its many forms and entertaining are but a few examples.

Those who risk their lives to entertain others such as racing drivers obtain immense pleasure from their work. The risk of death is, at times, very high, but this should never deter a determined person. If you really want to achieve something, you will do it regardless of the risk, for life on earth is full of hazard, especially in the home.

33

TYPICAL CASE HISTORIES

As an illustration of how people may reach a state of mental aberration that is totally baffling and unresponsive to the usual psychiatric approach, I shall present some more histories of actual cases from my files. I have been permanently appointed as advisor on psychiatric cases to the author.

The first case concerns a man in his twenties who, for the past five years, has been in the hands of social workers and psychiatrists. I shall give him the pseudonym of Raymond. He kept experiencing hallucinations and, on account of his condition, was forced to quit his job. His psychiatrist labelled him schizophrenic. As usual, he was given drugs which, if taken in sufficient quantity and frequently enough, resulted in a reduction of the incidents.

The drugs, though, also removed, almost entirely, his self-drive and he was unable to work or plan for the future. Convinced that he was insane, the young man hoped for the discovery of a new psychiatric technique that would rid him of his aberrated condition and allow him to stop taking drugs, upon which he was totally dependent.

Raymond first came to us in a very confused and bewildered state of mind. Heavily sedated by the drugs that he was taking, he was withdrawn and unable to confront us.

Through experience, we suspected that he was being influenced by a discarnate spiritual being and our first act upon meeting him was to scan the immediate vicinity for a strange spiritual being. It was easy to spot the stranger who, as expected, was standing some way off, afraid to approach more closely because of the presence of High Spiritual Beings.

He was instructed to come into the room, after Raymond had been interviewed. He was then questioned closely. He was of lower astral spiritual height, the lowest realm in heaven. When asked if he knew Raymond, he said he did and when interrogated firmly he admitted to having been responsible for Raymond's condition.

It appeared that our visitor, whom we shall call van Dongen, he gave his real name, hated his victim, now the subject of our case. In their previous lives, they were Boer farmers in the Transvaal and were neighbours and friends. Van Dongen, aged thirty when the Boer war began, was a descendant of the voortrekkers. They joined the Boer army and were trained to fight. Raymond was promoted to the rank of corporal and was placed in charge of a platoon of which van Dongen was a member.

While on patrol, the platoon was ambushed by the British, including an officer on horseback. Four of the platoon were killed and two taken prisoner, of whom van Dongen was one. Raymond disappeared. The prisoners were tortured by the British for information but they did not give anything away. Van Dongen was convinced that Raymond had deserted his platoon to save his own skin and he blamed him for the predicamemnt in which he, van Dongen, now found himself.

There follows a transcript of the recall of his previous incarnation given to Raymond by me, Carl Jung, after I had, earlier, studied the Akashic Record. During this method of recall, the recipient relaxes completely, preferably while lying down. The spiritual telepath then projects the image pictures retained in his own memory into the mind of the recipient.

Only those who are unsceptical and whose psychic awareness is awakened are able to receive recalls in this manner. This is what Raymond related.

"I see a horse under a tree in open country on the left hand side of my vision. A figure in black is standing on the right of the horse. A man approaches the horse. He has a big hat. He has mounted the horse. I thought for a moment the horse had fallen over but I am lying on my back. It is twilight. The picture is very clear. The man on the horse is dressed in dark clothing, black riding boots and a cloak. I can't see a uniform. He is having trouble with the horse. It is frisky. I feel as if I have been thrown off a horse; someone is stooping over me. He stands up and shakes his head. I can see a gun and soldiers. They've gone. I get up quickly.

It's getting darker. I feel for my revolver and wonder why they did not take it. I feigned death. Now I see a bungalow type house with a wooden front. I am feeling a lot better. Approaching the house from the side and looking through the window. I feel guilty about deserting my patrol and am only thinking of myself. I get the feeling of broken glass and am agitated. I am trying to get in through the window but I can't. All has gone quiet. My main thought is that I need a horse. I'm nervous of gunshots. I'm in a quandary. Can't find a horse. I'm in a panic. I need a horse. I start walking. It's a dark night and the stars are very bright. I can see rough country and rocky outcrops. I'm going along a track.

I sit down on a boulder and hold my head in my hands. I am shaking a bit and remorseful. I'm wiping my brow. Why didn't the British take my revolver? I check the cartridges and clean the gun, blowing out dust. I'm less nervous and thinking about my patrol but more concerned about myself. I've thrown the gun onto the ground. I don't know what to do. Now, I see lights, a bright light to the right. I am surrounded by friendly people who are shaking my hand. There are about six Boers. They are treating me as a hero. I'm laughing and smiling and we are hugging and kissing one another. I'm talking to them, gesticulating.

Someone points to my gun on the ground. I am afraid of handling it. It reminds me of the incident. I return the gun to my holster. I feel upset, now. There is a cart coming. We all get on it and drive away."

End of recall.

After the war, van Dongen died of natural causes, taking with him his hatred of Raymond whom he never forgave or forgot. The two men did not meet again but, only a few years after Raymond died in his previous incarnation, he was reincarnated. Either by chance or design, van Dongen located him while still in the spiritual world and began a vendetta against him. His technique was to stand close to Raymond and project random, unpleasant, telepathic messages into his mind. Raymond was spiritually low in any case and was an easy victim. He then began to doubt his own sanity. He consulted a doctor and was sent to a consultant psychiatrist with the results that have already been stated.

This method of implanting images into the minds of incarnate beings by people discarnate occurs commonly but, as with almost anything, it may be done with good intent or for evil purposes.

All great men and women are helped by the spiritual world if they are engaged in ethical and altruistic activities. The help is frequently, as in the case of an inventor, given by projecting

pictures or thoughts into the person's mind.   Usually, the recipient
believes that he thought of the images or ideas himself.

When used for evil, telepathy from the spiritual world to ours can
wreak havoc with the victim's reality of his environment, resulting in
paranoia. Unaware of the source of his mental troubles,he looks to the
psychiatric profession to prescribe a drug or to recommend a treatment
that he hopes will cure him.   Unfortunately, he is wasting his time
because, unless the source of the aberrations ceases his attacks upon
the victim's mind, there is no hope of a cure.

Drugs appear to diminish the effects of attacks because they are
anaesthetic to a greater or lesser degree and the mind is not able to
function normally through a brain that is under their influence.   In
this semi-conscious condition, telepathy is extremely ineffective. The
psychiatrist says to himself, "I have administered drug "x" to this
patient who claims that he is not hallucinating so severely or so
frequently, therefore the drug is improving his mental condition."
This is a false deduction. The drug merely prevents the telepathy from
being effective and, as soon as the patient stops taking it, he
relapses. The *only* cure for this very common cause of mental illness
is the removal of the source of the telepathic, aberrative thoughts
and mental image pictures.

In this particular case, van Dongen who was no better, nor
spiritually higher than a poltergeist, was told that he would be
reincarnated as a rat if he continued to molest Raymond.   He was then
shown some examples of humans who had been reincarnated as rats in the
Akashic record. This experience frightened van Dongen so much that he
completely changed his attitude towards Raymond and even offered to
help him in future.

Relieved of the cause of his mental problems, Raymond began to
improve and reduced his drug intake, gradually, until he found that he
was no longer dependent upon them. Exorcism, as commonly practised, is
unnecessary when a psychic with exceptional visual and telepathic
abilities is present because the offending spiritual being can be confronted and told that his continuing malpractice will have dire
results upon his kharma. This is usually sufficient.

The causes of psychosis in present time frequently have their
origins in former lives and the following is an actual, typical
example. In her current incarnation, our subject exhibited a normally
active academic mind. Her attitudes to others, though, were extremely
aberrated. These partly stemmed from the fact that her mother set a
very low example, especially in her derogatory attitude to the
subject's father, whom she treated, quite unjustifiably, with disdain
and apathy. Furthermore, her mother often repeated disparaging remarks
concerning boys, for whom she held a psychopathic antipathy. This mat-
ernal example had a profound effect upon the subject to whom I shall
give the pseudonym of Sarah.

With an already ingrained dislike of boys carried over from a
previous life, the last thing she wanted was reinforcement of it from
her mother.   Sarah married and her first-born child was a girl upon
whom she doted.   Her second child was a boy who was doomed, from the
moment his mother knew she had conceived again, to have hatred poured
upon him.   The result of her attitude to her son was the ruination of
the children's education and happiness and the virtual destruction of

36

her husband whose grief for his son's plight was of constant conceern and which affected him psychosomatically in numerous different ways.

Sarah became almost totally misanthropic. She was the only person who was ever right. All others were wrong. Her absolute intransigence and puerile obduracy finally wrecked the marriage. Fortunately, psychotics represent only a small minority but the repercussions of the disastrous effects that they have upon others are manifested in the misery and tragedy which they, oblivious of any guilt, have caused.

In her last incarnation, Sarah was a man and a tutor to the children of a well-to-do family in France at the time of the revolution. The tutor was very well treated and was paid for his services. His pupils were three boys and two girls whose ages ranged from five to twelve years. The two girls were the youngest and were very well behaved. The boys, by contrast, were prone to recalcitrancy and gave their tutor rather a troublesome time. One of their favourite pranks was to creep up behind him, whip off his wig and hide it. This, of course, provoked great hilarity amongst the servants who witnessed the tutor running breathlessly after the miscreants shouting threats of severe canings if his wig were not returned.

Owing to his total baldness, the tutor's vanity was severely shaken. Many other pranks were played on him by the three boys until he used to dread the coming of each new day. His resentment of the boys deepened as he felt his authority slipping away from him. The tutor's invalid wife, whom he loved dearly, needed medicines which were expensive but his wage was barely enough to keep them both enjoying the necessities of life. He dared not complain to the boy's parents who employed him because he knew that tutors were easily replaced.

Then his wife died leaving him grief-stricken and heartbroken. He became more and more bitter towards the boys who were now, emphatically, the bane of his existence and the last straw came when he was dismissed from his position by the family. Unable to find further employment, the man was forced to beg in the streets and finally he died of exposure and emaciation.

In her incarnation previous to the last one, Sarah was a girl in Florence, Italy in the year 1602. She was the tenth child of her catholic parents. They all lived in poverty and she had to suffer the additonal burden of being an unwanted child. Her daily routine consisted of housework and ministering to the needs of the younger children of the thirteen in the family.

The father, a simple peasant, worked for a mere pittance on a farm owned by a greedy, grasping landowner who exploited his workers. At the age of twelve, the girl was forced into prostitution by her parents and her earnings supplemented the limited family income. She was badly treated by some of her clients one of whom was the father of her baby boy whom she murdered by dropping him from a window onto the stone-flagged courtyard below. She did this because she felt unable to support the child. Sarah will continue to reincarnate until she loses her antagonism towards the male sex and her deep-rooted bitterness towards people. Between incarnations, she was shown her akashic record and was ashamed of her past but she did not seem to attach much importance to the fact that future incarnations were for the purposes of atonement and clearing her kharma.   As she appears to scorn all offers of help,   she must atone in her own time and will continue to reap as she sows.

The next case concerns a young boy whose wild and irresponsible behaviour had led to his being sent to a special school.   His parents were unable to cope with him, although their other children were perfectly normal. The lad held a deep resentment of any kind of authority and frequently stole from shops with an apparent unawareness that he was guilty of an offence.   Psychiatrists who had examined the boy, whom I shall call William, could find no obvious cause of his unsocial behaviour.   His intelligence was found to be slightly above average but, owing to a hearing impediment, he had earlier been regarded as backward , particularly in reading. While being taught to read, William could not hear the way the teacher was pronouncing the words and was unable to relate the sound to the written word.

William's akashic record of his present life shows that he has been often invalidated, particularly by his teachers. He has seldom received credit for that which he did well.   This has driven him down to apathy and, in that condition, he accepts no responsibility for his own actions.

The basic causes of William's erratic and unconcerned behaviour lie, however, mainly in his last life.   Born a German, William was forced to join the Hitler youth movement against his will.   He then volunteered for the Luftwaffe at the outbreak of the second world war and was trained as a pilot. He participated in a number of raids over London in a Heinkel bomber and was highly decorated for his courage in action.

Towards the end of the war, William was promoted to the rank of Oberst or colonel and was placed in command of bomber squadrons oper-ating on the Russian front.   Having a philosophical approach to life, he was appalled at the suffering that surrounded him daily and fervently wished that Hitler had never been born.

During a Russian attack on an airfield which the colonel was visiting, he was captured and taken to Russia for interrogation. While there, he was brainwashed and subjected to intensive psychological "treatment" in an attempt to force him to disclose information about the Luftwaffe's intentions and capabilities. Unable to make him disclose anything, the Russian torturers then proceeded to inflict upon the colonel such indignities as making him stand naked in the snow and depriving him of his clothing when in his cell.   Still determined not to crack, and displaying inordinate courage, he was, finally, treated so cruelly that he died from the effects.

William has been reincarnated as an Englishman in order to show him that national pride and hatred of other nations and races are pointless.   So vivid is his subconscious memory of his last life that he distrusts everyone around him. By behaving outrageously at home and at school William merely thinks that he is demonstrating his independence. He does not see why he should not steal because his subconscious memory contains numerous incidents where he was personally responsible for enormous destruction and loss of life. For creating such havoc and suffering, he was formerly rewarded.   Now, no one rewards him and he fails to understand why.

William is atoning for crimes committed in earlier lives than his last and it would appear that he is not going to have an easy time, neither will anyone who comes into contact with him. Provided this lad is given the same treatment and discipline as any other boy of comparable behaviour, his characteristics of self-determinism, individuality, adventurousness and indomitable courage should, ultimately, ensure his success, both in career and kharma.

Although able to display considerable understanding of the spiritual existence, an acquaintance of the author simply refused to accept reincarnation. From experience, I knew that she was trying to hide her past and to pretend to herself that it did not happen. Wishing to help her, we checked on her akashic record and this is what we found.

Two centuries and three lives ago our friend was a Chinese "hill soldier". An officer and a man, he was as utterly ruthless with his own men as he was with the enemy soldiers. He frequently had his own men beheaded for trivial reasons such as their misunderstanding an order. After a battle, a certain number of prisoners were kept so that he, personally, could torture them to death. The remainder were slaughtered on his command.

In the life following that one our subject, having expressed horror at his previous behaviour, reincarnated as a woman. She suffered terribly from poverty, starvation and a brutal husband. Upon returning yet again to heaven, the spiritual being studied really hard and tried to improve. She was successful in reaching Plane Two.

In her subsequent life, once more as a woman, she endured even more suffering but after her death she again applied herself diligently to study and attained the spiritual height of Plane Three, from which she was born into her present life, again as a woman. Through atonement and suffering, our subject has worked her way up to Plane Four. This particular person is fortunate because there is a strong likelihood that she will not reincarnate and her experiences are a good example of a successful climb upwards from the depths of depravity. Without a strong desire to abandon her earlier love of iniquity, however, she would never have made the grade.

The next case is a perfect example of present-life problems, the causes of which originated almost one thousand years ago. A middle aged woman explained that she was very agoraphobic, suffered a morbid fear of rape not only of herself but of her two daughters also and experienced a marked antipathy towards anyone or anything Chinese.

The Akashic Record showed that, in the tenth century, the woman was the daughter of a Chinese mandarin. Lacking no creature comforts, So-Lei, as she was then known, enjoyed a privileged existence even to the extent of being waited upon by servants.

Disaster struck the family when So-Lei had reached the age of fourteen years when brigands ruthlessly invaded her home and murdered her parents before her eyes. She was raped by five of the bandits in turn but the sixth man, apparently not totally devoid of feeling for others, took pity on the screaming, helpless young girl being held down before him. He felt ashamed of the way the innocent girl, still a child, was being treated and drew a knife ordering his companions to release her. Somewhat surprised, the brigands released So-Lei and then ransacked the house, stealing everything that they could carry. The sixth man whose name was Pak Wong carried the girl to his horse and rode off with her into the hills where, in a well-hidden cave, he gave her food and drink.

Owing to the moral standards impressed upon her by her family, So-Lei felt that, having lost her virginity in such a manner, she had forfeited the right to live and she grabbed at Pak Wong's knife in order to kill herself. He was too quick for her, though, and snatched it out of her reach.

After refreshment and rest, the man explained that he wanted to abandon his marauding life. They journeyed for many days until they came upon a village by the sea. As they waited for two days in the hills overlooking the village, watching the occupants and assessing the situation, So-Lei began to trust the brigand who was treating her kindly and with respect. Finally, Pak Wong decided to take a chance and try to settle in the village.

They were eyed with much suspicion at first, but Pak Wong explained that they had been travelling for many days after having escaped from a gang of brigands. His story was accepted, and some villagers took pity on the young girl.

For a long time So-Lei moped over her fate and, believing herself unworthy of him, refused to marry Pak Wong. The suspicions of the villagers were aroused and their constant peeping through the door of her hut finally decided her to consent to marriage. Two daughters resulted from the marriage, both of whom are the woman's daughters in her present life.

The traumatic experiences of that earlier incarnation burned deeply into her subconscious mind. The awful fear of travelling in unknown, open and dangerous terrain with a villain, even though he did not behave like one to her, has left its mark in present time in the form of agoraphobia.

The origin of her pathological dread of rape is plain to see and, of course, anything Chinese acts as a restimulation of the deep-seated engrams that were implanted in her subconscious mind one thousand years ago.

One of the most significant factors that can induce a state of aberration is the engram. An engram may be defined as the subliminal retention of sensory and emotional perceptions in the subconscious mind during moments when the person is not fully conscious. In order for the induced engram to have an effect on the person it must, at a later time, be re-awakened.

Contrary to popular belief, an unconscious person, instead of being totally unaware, is in fact recording in the subconscious mind every aspect of his environment including body position, temperature, sounds and even the dialogue of people in the vicinity. While the conscious mind is closed down, the subconscious mind is opened up so that everything in one's environment is being recorded.

The insidious manner in which the engram works has to be experienced for it to be thoroughly understood. Furthermore, time is irrelevant in this context and, while most people suffer to some extent from engrams received in their present life, including their

40

birth engram, many are also being affected by incidents that occurred in previous lives, sometimes centuries or even millennia ago.

The most common causes of engrams are total anaesthetics, severe accidents of any kind, highly traumatic experiences such as war and any incident that leaves the person in a state of shock. The cause of the shock does not have to be physical. Mental distress, on learning of the death of a close friend or relative can also partially close down the conscious mind, thus opening up the subconscious mind in proportion.

Engrams may contain pain, emotion, grief, anxiety, fear, sympathy and a sense of loss or remorse, either singly or in combination.

Unless he is fully acquainted with the mechanism of the engram, the victim remains unaware of the cause of his present-time problem because it lies in the past in a section of the mind that, in normal circumstances, is inaccessible to the conscious mind.

Probably, the easiest way to explain the functioning of engrams is to give some examples and, since the author has experienced a number of his own, I shall ask him to relate some of them here.

After joining the Royal Air Force at the age of sixteen years, I was expected to have my hair cut at very frequent intervals as the "short back and sides" was the style insisted upon. This, in itself, was of little consequence but, every time that it became my turn to sit in the barber's chair, I began to feel faint. Fortunately, I never actually fainted but the feeling was very strong and it caused me considerable embarrassment and concern. During my adult RAF service, I experienced the phenomenon every time that I had my hair cut but to a lesser degree. It was not until I had left the Service and had reached the age of thirty-three, that I discovered the cause of my problem.

Eric, a good friend of mine was, in addition to being a good pianist and a fellow musician, also searching for the answers to man's existence and behaviour. He used a simple, verbal abreaction technique on me. We discovered that it was possible, merely by guidance, to direct my mind back to the moments when I had picked up engrams in my present life. While I was being conducted backwards in time, scanning my own subconscious mind, I encountered one or two minor incidents and then I found myself seated in a dentist's chair.

Relating my experiences continuously to my friend, I said, "I am having a tooth filled. I am nine years old. The dentist is drilling a tooth in my lower left jaw having administered no anaesthetic. I have fainted and am lolling over the left side of the chair. The dentist has put down his drill and is sitting me up. I dazedly come round, feeling very giddy and with an aching jaw". On hearing this, my friend realised that we had struck an engram and so asked me to repeat the whole incident several times. Finally, it became immediately obvious that here was the cause of the problem in the hairdresser's chair.

On analysis, it was perfectly evident that the environment was almost identical with the engram environment. The chair was leather-covered and adjustable for height and back angle, there was a white, porcelain sink with a tumbler on it, shiny metal tools lay around, a man in a white coat was bending over me and water was running. As far as the engrammic content of my subconscious mind was concerned, the barber's shop was no different from the dental surgery. From the day

41

when I re-experienced this engram, I have never again felt that I was going to faint when sitting in a barber's chair.   The cause had been discovered, recognised and transferred from the subconscious mind to the conscious mind where it remains as only an innocuous memory entirely lacking any power to affect me in future.

By the end of the Second World War, my nerves were in a poor state. My duties in the Royal Air Force consisted of ensuring that fighter aircraft went into combat with fully functioning radio equipment. Deeply involved in the Battle of Britain as a ground maintenance airman, I served in turn on 17 Squadron Hurricanes and 602 City of Glasgow Squadron Spitfires at Debden, Martlesham Heath, Croydon, Kenley and Redhill.   While on leave at my parents' home in South-East London, the nightly bombing raids caused a surfeit of adrenalin to flow.

Upon my return to Debden, the RAF camp became a prime target of the Luftwaffe and was bombed twice in one week causing extensive damage to the buildings with the loss of about twelve lives.   Four hundred bombs were dropped, all inside the camp area.

As I was about to enter the underground air-raid shelter during the first raid, a bomb exploded at the entrance to the "H" block and the blast blew me down the steps while glass crashed around me from the ablution area.

At Martlesham, the camp was raided in full daylight by a string of six Dornier 17's while we stood in a virtually useless air-raid shelter. A bombed-up Fairey Battle aircraft received a direct hit and blew up. A social evening in nearby Ipswich was interrupted by the German raiders.

In 1943 I volunteered to serve with 124 Wing of the Second Tactical Air Force, knowing that it would be spearheading the imminent invasion of Europe.

Typhoons and Tempests constitutued the aircraft of 247, 181 and 182 Squadrons on each of which I served at some time . "D" Day came on June 6th, 1944 and within ten days I was under canvas in Normandy near the village of Coulombs on B6 Airfield, a hastily-constructed landing strip.

The rocket-firing Typhoons flew all the daylight hours culminating in the destruction of the German forces in the Falaise gap. The occasional lone German fighter plane strafed our aircraft on the ground.   Only two kilometres from the front line, we were surrounded by the constant noise of the British heavy guns while ahead of us we heard the "crump" of German shells.   Day and night, this went on for weeks.

We were deprived of sleep at night by the lone nuisance raider who circled above our airfield drawing anti-aircraft fire from the army, the RAF Regiment and even the Royal Navy patrolling the English Channel only a few kilometres north of us. The flak seemed to be concentrated over B6 Airfield and, as we lay under the useless protection of a canvas tent, we heard the shell fragments hissing through the trees in our dispersal area hitting the ground with a cracking noise.

When our forces broke away from the Caen area, I drove my three-ton Crossley containing the Signals workshop, in convoy.   Things were a little quieter from then on until we installed our Wing at Eindhoven airfield in Holland.

As Eric guided me further and further back in time, I squirmed in my chair. "What is happening?" asked Eric. "I am in a cinema in Southend with my wife. It is 1948. We are watching "Rommel, Desert Fox" I said. The El Alamein barrage is being depicted. The guns are too loud. The screen is covered with flashes. I am beginning to tremble and shake. I feel terrible. If I do not leave the auditorium, I feel as though I may break down, so I am going to the "Gents"."

After about twenty minutes during which time I felt awful, unable to control the shaking, my stomach aching, I returned to my seat. It was many days later before I recovered from this experience. Realising that I had struck a particularly heavy engram because of the distress that I exhibited during my retelling of the incident, Eric asked me to run through it again.

During the second running, I had reached the point where I was watching the El Alamein bombardment when, suddenly, I said, "I am not in the cinema. I am in Eindhoven. It is January 1st, 1945, New Year's Day. I am lying on ice on a small dyke under some trees. Cannon and machine gun fire are all around. Every now and again, there is a loud explosion."

Now I realised where all the fear and grief originated. It was this raid, the final fling of Goering's Luftwaffe, during which our Wing suffered many casualties in twenty-one minutes. They were, without doubt, the most traumatic twenty-one minutes of my life so far. Caught in bed at 0900 hours, at first I thought we were under a land attack. Then, it seemed like a bombing raid but, wasting no time, I leapt off my chicken-wire bed in the sixteen degrees below zero temperature in the former bomb store that we were using as a billet, pulled on my trousers, grabbed my rifle and steel helmet and ran outside. Looking left, I was gazing straight at the blazing barrels of a Focke-Wulf 190 as it strafed just above my head. I dashed into the copse ahead and sought shelter. There was nothing but a few sparsely distributed silver birch trees. The noise was deafening.

Thirty Focke-Wulf 190's and Messerschmidt 109's were circling our airfield. They had destroyed the bomb dump used by a Canadian Wing sharing our airfield. I was freezing in my half-dressed condition, dazed and shocked but, finally, the din subsided.

This experience, the culmination of a series of horrifying experiences accumulated during five years of war, had left me with a massive war engram. Any film of war was likely to re-awaken it, as was any sudden loud noise such as a jet aircraft passing low overhead or any sound resembling an explosion.

As I worked at an airfield, I was continually in a provocative environment. This had a disastrous effect on my general health and I developed a number of chronic psychosomatic illnesses as a result.

Near my house was an army firing range and several times I was awakened from my sleep at around midnight by a simulated war with bombs, guns and machine guns impinging upon my subconscious mind. At first, I thought I was still involved in the war then it slowly dawned on me that it was the army holding a night exercise. Eric, my patient friend, helped me through many present-life engrams with the result

43

that my health began to improve. During this period, I learned a great deal about the workings of the mind and the causes of psychomatic illnesses.

Some years later, I had discovered that I was still being affected by engrams that I had received in earlier lives. During an examination of one of these, I found that I had fought as a cannonier as an Englishman with the Hanoverian army at Culloden in 1746 during the suppression of the Jacobite rebellion in Scotland. There was considerable emotion in this engram but many more years passed before I was to experience an abreaction in a most spectacular and dramatic way.

Seated next to my wife on a settee one evening, we were watching an American film of the Second World War. Until about half way, all was well but then some men were walking down a hill when they came under attack from a shell barrage. It had no sooner commenced than I began to feel ill at ease. This feeling rapidly increased until I was distraught and trying to indicate to my wife that I wanted the television switched off. So choked with emotion was I that speech was impossible.

For several minutes I was unable to answer my wife's repeated requests to explain what was the matter. She, not unnaturally, thought that I had been taken suddenly ill. Then, the awful truth hit me. I was reliving my experiences at Culloden in 1746.

When I finally managed to explain to my wife, she understood immediately and knew exactly what to do. She had been relieved of some of her engrams by me some years before. She patiently guided me through the incidents while I was pouring out grief that had remained locked in my sub-conscious mind for two hundred and thirty-two years.

At the lowered sword of my gunnery officer, I fired my cannon, a massive piece and the largest in the battle. The effect of the cannon balls on the lines of Scotsmen was frightful and I do not intend to give all the bloody details here.

After the Scots, outnumbered and inferiorly trained, had been beaten, I went with other soldiers to loot the bodies of the dead. Ahead of me, our soldiers were bayonetting the enemy wounded.

During the relating of this ghastly event, I was in an intense state of grief, at times unable to speak. After two and a half hours, the engram-trapped emotion began to recede and I lapsed into a state of almost total exhaustion. My wife, too, was depleted after such a gruelling session.

The entire battle of Culloden, as seen by me, and the chases and the skirmishing that followed it were all described by me in vivid detail as though it had only happened the previous day.

Of course, at the time, I showed no outward sign to my fellow soldiers as to how deeply the event had affected me and I was probably unaware of the extent of the trauma in any case.

I, Carl Jung, shall end this chapter by reiterating the urgently vital need for all those engaged in dealing with the mental and emotional problems of others to study deeply and seriously the spiritual existence. They must throw aside professional bigotry and deviate from clinical practices, being prepared to start anew their education regarding the true nature of man and his mind.

CHAPTER SIX

DEATH DEFINED

Current theological thought represents a primitive state of spiritual awareness based as it is upon data that were either originally false or have been falsified later. While claiming to minister to the spiritual welfare of millions, the clergy ultimately bring chaos and confusion to the minds of their congregations by dogmatically feeding them heavy and repeated doses of misleading information based almost entirely upon ancient writings and the erroneous interpretations of them by priests and theological scholars.

Unable to substantiate any of their claims by virtue of personal knowledge or experience, their only recourse is to teach, parrot fashion, that which they were taught and which, unfortunately, they were unable to evaluate correctly by using their own God-given powers of discernment.

As an example of this, an archbishop, writing about God, attempts to define Him and His attitudes to man but where he claims that God retains the greatest punishment of all for the biggest sinners, death, he is utterly wrong, since death is seldom a punishment and in a great many cases is a deliberately-given reward.

The release from the pain, suffering, trials and tribulations of life incarnate on earth to a higher plane in heaven is infinitely better and more desirable than decaying in helpless senility, with the accompanying miseries that old age can bring, particularly to those of limited means or poor general health.

Death then, far from being a punishment is frequently a liberation, a promotion for a life well lived, an accolade. It is often the manner of death that constitutes the atonement or punishment for earlier sins hence the hundreds of different kinds of death that people do suffer but death itself should never be regarded as a punishment imposed by God.

One's span on earth is determined before birth and only in exceptional circumstances does God alter people's kharmas by returning them to heaven before their appointed time as a reward or by keeping them incarnate as an atonement.

Why is death such a subject for fear by the majority of people? Firstly, the instinct to survive in corporeal form is deeply entrenched in the mind from the moment of incarnation onward. This is essential, otherwise people might regard life in physical bodies as something less than desirable with an inevitable increase in deaths by carelessness, accidents and suicide. The carefully planned kharmas of such people would be ruined and they would only have to reincarnate yet again in order to compensate for the atonement lost by an earlier than planned demise.

Secondly, people know subconsciously why they are on earth and the thought is always at the back of the mind of the person carrying a heavy burden of guilt concerning his crimes in former lives that he is going to have to confront his past, yet again, after death. We all have to do that but it is not surprising that those with a particularly horrible past are reluctant to be reminded of it.

Thirdly, not one in a thousand people knows the truth about death.

Those who do, lose all fear of it because when something is thoroughly understood it cannot be feared. Jesus Christ said, "Perfect love casteth out fear", and that is true, but it is also true that perfect understanding casts out fear.

If more people understood death it would cease to be an occasion for mourning, grief and misery and would become as welcome a topic as birth is.

Well, what *is* death? It is the transition of a spiritual being incarnate to one discarnate. The physical body which is on loan, so to speak, for the duration of one's earthly life, is only a vehicle for the spiritual mind and body and, when it ceases to operate at death, the spiritual being continues, unaltered, to exist in the spiritual world.

What is it like to die? The actual transition from physical life to purely spiritual life is quite painless and is, frequently, a moment of great happiness. The encumbering weight of the physical body falls away. One feels light and often experiences a floating sensation as one moves upward. All pain, if there had been any, ceases. This departure from the earthly shell may be compared with passing through a doorway or, more accurately, a veil. This veil, at the moment of death, is a thin one and many people are hardly aware of it. So tenuous is it that some who have passed through it cannot believe or accept that they have died and try to carry on as they did on earth. The latter are usually materialistic in outlook and have no understanding of their spiritual reality.

Finally, to quote the great Carl Jung, "One should look forward to one's death with the same joyful anticipation as one looks forward to next week."

After the silver cord has been severed, there can be no return to the physical body. Helpers on the other side receive the newly returned spiritual being and, if the passing has been sudden or painful, they take the person to a reception centre. There are several of these and they resemble hospitals.

The new arrival is left in a bed to sleep until the shock and other effects have subsided. Then he is told that he has died and is assured that there is nothing to worry about.

If the person is on a higher plane he will usually proceed directly to that plane and if his passing was peaceful there is no need for a rest and recovery period. Instead, he will be reintroduced to the heavenly world that he knew before his last incarnation. Relatives that one may not have seen, since their passing many years earlier, greet the newcomer and explain the rules of existence in the unaccustomed environment. From then on, the spiritual progress and the knowledge and understanding that the spiritual being achieves depend entirely upon him.

One has only to attend a Christian funeral service to discover how little the priests know about death. They quote from the gospels but have little spiritual comfort to offer the bereaved, yet they officiate at people's passing and do not understand it.

The Christian belief that the dead shall lie in their graves until the last day of judgment, when they will be resurrected, indicates a total lack of knowledge or understanding. The last day? What is that? When will it be? It has not happened yet, after millions of years.

This useless information is the best that Christianity can offer anyone grieving at the loss of a dear one. It is not good enough. When one considers the wide range of books written posthumously on the subject of death it is surprising that more people do not know more about it. Catholics go so far as to forbid cremation because, otherwise, how could the body be resurrected if it had been burnt? Compare this idiosyncracy with their belief that heretics must be burnt alive to save them from eternal hell fire.

Burial of bodies takes up large areas of ground that could be put to better use. Unfortunately, most people believe that the body *is* the the person, hence the costly and elaborate memorials that are erected and, in many cases, the numerous visits to the grave.

The only valid memorial to departed loved ones is in the memory of them. Those who, in their grief, make regular visits to a grave are exhibiting a highly materialistic approach to death. If they were only psychic enough they might even be able to see the lost one standing beside them trying hard to explain that he is not dead, but still very much alive.

Grief has a very adverse psychomatic effect upon the person who suffers it. It can do nobody any good, least of all the subject of one's grief because he or she should be free to forget about the earthly existence and concentrate upon spiritual progress. I can speak with assurance about grief for I have known its darkest depths. That was before I came into the knowledge and it occurred during the nadir of my present life.

It is perfectly natural to feel a deep sense of loss after having lived with the person just departed for the best part of a lifetime but one should be able to come to terms with this by accepting that there is no death. Grief is, in reality, an expression of self-pity.

If only people understood that it is far better to exist in heaven than on earth, then their entire approach to death would change. As I have spoken with scores of people in the spiritual world, I have never met one who really wanted to return to earth. Those who know that they must do so usually accept the fact philosophically but seldom with enthusiasm.

The darkness of men's minds on earth is in deep contrast with the brilliance that surrounds one while discarnate, with the exception of the lower astral plane which is a place of perpetual gloom reflecting as it does the mental outlook and spiritual state of its occupants.

CHAPTER SEVEN

CHRIST REVEALS HIMSELF

Communication with the spiritual world has been going on for many centuries but there are certain principles governing such communication that must be adhered to before accurate, two-way contact may be established with the highest spiritual beings in heaven of whom God and Jesus Christ are but two.

High Spiritual Beings are quite unable to communicate with people on earth unless those people are spiritually high and, in addition, have an excellent understanding of the realities of life, life after death, and heaven. If one considers this long enough it must be seen to be true. The situation may be compared with a hypothetical example whereby a university don is asked to explain the quantum theory to a class of infants.

So it is with people like Jesus Christ. Because He is not the being that all Christian religions make Him out to be, He is unable to establish good communication with anyone who believes that He is God or that He died for their sins or was born of a virgin and these are the basic articles of faith of Christianity. It then becomes obvious that the last person on earth with whom Jesus Christ *could* communicate even if He wanted to is a Christian.

Let us suppose that Jesus Christ were to attempt to communicate through a medium who is religiously orientated towards Him. Owing to the fact that telepathic communication utilises the minds of both the sender and receiver of the message, the result would be twisted beyond recognition and, although the medium may well be aware of who is sending the intelligence, his own preconceptions and misconceptions would ensure that the statements were peppered with religious jargon.

Consider any statements made in the past by people claiming to have received direct communication from God. Are they not all couched in religious terms? Does not the language of the church predominate? Of course it does; because even if the recipient *is* receiving information from the spiritual world, the conditioned mind of the medium causes him to receive messages as he would expect to receive them.

This said, it can be seen that the *only* way that correct communication could be received from a spiritual being of Jesus Christ's spiritual height is through a medium who is not steeped in religion and whose mind is open to receive the truth however much it might differ from the widely-accepted beliefs that masquerade as truths in religions.

My experience in the spiritual field of study led me to make many observations concerning the nature of existence which have since been corroborated by the highest authorities in heaven. Never, even as a child, having been able to accept the religious view of Jesus Christ, I was nevertheless fascinated by the mystery surrounding His existence. A detailed study of the four gospels during my twenties led me to conclude that, on the basis of the evidence contained in them, Christ had been rescued alive from the tomb.

Of course, I had no way of determining how, or the identity of His rescuers, because, although it is recorded in the gospels, the descriptive language of the time cannot be fully understood without a good understanding of the true nature of the spiritual phenomena that were being observed.

My wife, Amanda, and I had been communicating by spirit writing for several weeks and had been holding very sensible conversations with our departed relatives and friends. Then, I realised that a man who called himself Abe came every day to speak with me. He told me that he had been Jewish in his last incarnation, and that he lived recently in Israel. After some time had elapsed, it occurred to me to ask if he were my spiritual guide, to which he answered, "Yes". Whereupon, I plied Abe with questions about life, death, life in heaven, other planets and numerous other subjects that were seething around in my mind seeking answers. The explanations that Abe gave me were, sometimes very illuminating and even astounding but, at that time, I had received no verification, from other sources, of his statements. Since then, I most certainly have done and everything that he told me was true.

One evening, I was receiving spirit writing, sometimes misnamed automatic writing, from my, by now, very good friend Abe as this technique of communication had become quite facile. I asked Abe if he knew the truth about Jesus Christ and he said that he did. My next question was, "Have you met Him?" Again, the answer was, "Yes".

Perhaps I was prompted but I then said, "Is He there?" My surprise and amazement can be imagined when I was informed that Jesus Christ was present in the spiritual world and also in my room.

Taking my courage in both hands, my next question was, "Could I, please, speak to Him?" There was a pause of about twenty seconds after which my pen began to move across the paper in an obviously different style from Abe's. This is what appeared before me.

"Good evening to you, Alan, my dear friend. I am Jesus Christ of Nazareth and Calvary. You are now in a state of grace. You have done well in this life and have reached a degree of understanding never before achieved by anyone on earth. I wish you to work for us by using your talents in spiritual matters. We shall guide you and, if you accept this challenge, you will be very well rewarded. First, though, you will be tested because we cannot work with anyone on earth until they have shown that they accept us completely and indicate a deep understanding of us. You are free to decline the work that we offer you because it will be arduous and very demanding but if your answer is, "No", then you will be on your own again and will receive no more help from us."

I could hardly believe what was happening to me. I was delighted at the incredible fact that the great man was writing to me but, at the same time, I must confess to having felt somewhat overawed. The almost casual way in which the communication occurred and the entire absence of any "holy talk" put me at my ease after the initial excitement had worn off and I proceeded to ask Jesus Christ some pertinent questions about Himself.

As I was tiring, He wrote that He would write to me again the next day. Nearly falling over myself, I ran downstairs to tell my wife about my most recent communicant.

From this time onwards, Jesus Christ visited us every day. He has written many wonderful scripts through both Amanda and me. He has elucidated His purpose in reincarnating and has explained what really occurred during the numerous outwardly miraculous events of His life. The analysis and appraisal of Christianity in this book have been approved by Jesus Christ in person as He is only too pleased to be able to set the record straight once and for all.

He has told us of the bitter disappointment felt by ardent Christians when they arrive back in heaven, after their passing. They do not walk straight into His arms as many are led to believe, neither do they find themselves in God's realms. On the contrary, owing to the fact that they have filled their minds with totally false beliefs about God, Jesus Christ, the so-called Holy Virgin Mary, the saints, angels, cherubs, the non-existent forgiveness of sins and so on and so on, they find that they are, once more, at the bottom of the class spiritually.

What follows may be many more incarnations on earth before they can drop their adherence to religions, in addition to concentrated study under knowledgeable tutors in heaven between lives.

The higher the rank of the clergy, the farther they fall after death and the sight of a totally bewildered and disillusioned pope or archbishop after his return to the *lowest* plane in heaven is a pathetic one to behold. So confident are they that they have been chosen by God to lead their followers to salvation that the shock of learning that, in heaven, they are of no importance at all is, frequently, more than they can bear.

At first, the newly returned cleric may be arrogant and may demand to see Jesus Christ or God but the helpers in heaven, appointed to explain what has happened to the person, patiently explain that what the churchmen believed in and taught others was entirely false.

It invariably takes a long time for this to sink in. After all, a lifetime's convictions invalidated and reduced to nought can only leave the holder of those persuasions floundering in a sea of confusion.

As the initial trauma of the situation begins to wear off, the former zealot sinks into a state of apathy, unless he is sensible enough to accept the situation and the challenge with which he is confronted, in which case he will be given all assistance to rid his mind of the cloying tenets of orthodoxy .

The deeper the convictions of the prelates and other religious people, the more difficult it is to substitute truth for belief.

Probably the most difficult task facing the guides, tutors and instructors in heaven is that of trying to convince millions of religiously-minded spiritual beings that what they were taught is wrong and then putting them on the right path, the one that, finally, leads to an understanding of the truth.

This path is long, tortuous and strewn with obstacles but it is the only route to the highest planes in heaven where both God and Jesus Christ can be found engaged in their perpetual work on behalf of spiritual beings both incarnate and discarnate.

It would enormously simplify the work of the people in heaven if only the individuals on earth would think more for themselves rather than believing everything that they are told by others. All persons have the ability and the right to think for themselves. They must do so if ever the rot of religion is going to be stopped, and stopped it must be, before the legitimate aims of its practitioners can be turned

into a reality.   Salvation, to Christians, means   reaching a state
where they are no longer encumbered by the unpleasant repercussions of
sinful behaviour. *Only* by becoming "de-religionised" can anyone reach
that quintessential paradise towards which they strive but which they
fail to attain through their religious beliefs and practices.

This is the universal irony! Those who claim to be able to issue
passports to the Kingdom of Heaven cannot do it through the teaching
and practices of their churches.   God has no church. Think about it!
Which one would He be able to choose of the thousands on earth?   They
cannot all be right. Only one religion could possibly be right but, in
fact, none is right.

Not only are the religions wrong in their assumptions but they
cause great harm to their adherents by feeding them false information
that fits them ill for their ultimate departure from earth. As already
explained, the time spent on religious study could well be put to
better use. It is infinitely better to contemplate the course of one's
own life and to assess one's own behaviour than to accept well-meant
but usually totally misguided advice from priests who, in reality,
know absolutely nothing of the truth of the spiritual existence and
whose actual power is zero in Godly terms.

There is no need to belong to a church or to hold strong
convictions about any religion in order to follow the examples of
humanitarianism that have been set by the great men of the past such
as Christ and Albert Schweitzer to name but two.

If everyone tried to model his life on the principles of Albert
Schweitzer alone he could not fail to succeed.   This does not imply
that everyone should dash off to darkest Africa as a medical
missionary but it does mean that, while keeping the lofty ideals of
this great man in mind, they should strive to emulate his selflessness
and devotion to the welfare of others, even at their own expense in
time and sometimes money. They can do this while still working at
their own job or enjoying an outside recreational activity or a hobby.

The natural and desirable sequel to the acquisition of skill and
knowledge is for it to be passed on to others. One of the best ways of
gaining, spiritually, is to learn an art and then to devote much time
to handing on one's knowledge to others who are interested.

Where there is an element of risk such as in the sports of flying,
skiing and underwater swimming, for example, the devoted instructor
can, by virtue of his or her concern for the students' safety, be in-
strumental in preventing them from making errors that could result in
their being injured or even killed.

The instructors in these demanding sports must often forgo their
own pleasures in order to devote enough time to training others, but,
in the long run, they benefit spiritually far more than those who are
content simply to take everything out of the sporting organisation
without ever contributing anything.

It is not necessary to become an ascetic or to impose rigorous
disciplines upon oneself such as drinking only water and converting to
vegetarianism. Anyone can, by turning his attention away from himself
and showing a genuine concern for others, do himself far more good in
a short time than he would in a lifetime of religious practice.

Many people are gregarious to an extreme degree, however, and are
not able to exhibit their individuality. Unless they are surrounded by

their group of friends upon whose characteristics their own behaviour is modelled, they feel lost.

The purely materialistic pursuits such as lechery and regular drunkenness only retard a person's progress. The enjoyment of sex and the intake of alcohol are not sins but excessive indulgence in any carnal pleasure can become a sin against oneself.

The results to a being's kharma of his becoming addicted to drugs are frightful. The indescribable damage to his mind may take many lifetimes to be healed. The drop-out not only drops out of his own society because of his reluctance to accept any form of discipline combined with his decision that the older generations are ignorant but upon his return to heaven he finds himself in a terrible emotional condition.

Remember, a spiritual being, incarnate or otherwise, is the end product of his own thoughts and attitudes. "As a man thinks, so is he." It is incumbent upon every person on earth to guard himself against the firm establishment of extreme ideas in his mind for extremism leads always to trouble. Moderation, especially in one's approach to one's fellow beings is most highly desirable.

Millions of people sincerely desire to do well in life, hence the impressive voluntary membership of the churches but their good intentions frequently come to naught because they are willing to accept an extreme religion. Their total acceptance of the creed of the church, they are informed, automatically ensures their salvation and a high place in heaven. Alas, it does not. Far from it.

Only the individual person can save or redeem himself. No Messiah or so-called saviour can possibly do it for him. All that they can do is to set the example for others to follow.

Passing the responsibility for one's own shortcomings and behaviour onto others is a popular habit of religious people.

It can be observed that few people are willing to accept responsibility for their own behaviour. It is they and they alone who *are* responsible though and that fact is made manifestly obvious to them after their departure from earth and their return to heaven.

If the bible alone is the source of one's inspiration, then it *is* possible to isolate and interpret some of the concepts that, if put into practice, would raise a person spiritually but it is the utterly confusing numinous terminology associated with the ritualistic character of most churches that renders it extremely difficult, if not impossible, to bring the implementation of those concepts to a point of fructuation.

It does not take the average child long to learn right from wrong and because, deep in the sub-conscious mind, the young person has a built-in knowledge of why he is on earth and what he must do to fulfil his kharma, it is instinctive to behave correctly. Why then do so many choose the evil path? Because, even though they know they are doing wrong, they enjoy it.

Sadism is an extreme example of pleasure gained at the expense of another's pain and suffering. The sadist knows that he is committing a crime but he just does not care and is oblivious of the incredible harm that he is doing to himself which, frequently, outweighs the harm done to his victim. A person who is sadistic in one of his lives will always have to reincarnate in order to atone for his sins but even in his next life he may lapse into his former evil ways although, before his birth, he may have sworn that he would conquer his aberration.

There are numerous spiritual beings who reincarnate full of good intentions, having been horrified at their behaviour in former lives, only to repeat the same sins. The murderer will murder again, the suicide will take his life yet again, the rapist and the thief will continue to exercise their will and thwart their kharmas.

Some spiritual beings live very many lifetimes before they become able and willing to abandon the paths of wickedness. Yet others, having been sinful in their previous life, manage to wipe out those sins and clean their kharmic slates by fulfilling their intended destinies.

It is these latter who climb the spiritual ladder successfully and whose well-being and joy increase to the extent that they succeed; for the greatest, most joyous experience of all awaits everyone on the higher planes in heaven.

CHAPTER EIGHT

EXEGESIS

As, at the time of writing, there is no known organisation that possesses the truth, the reader will, undoubtedly, be wondering how the present author can exhibit such irreverend temerity as to criticise the established churches' beliefs and teachings especially as they concern the central figure and foundation stone of the religion, Jesus Christ.

According to the beliefs of many, such a heathen, indulging in what they would term blasphemy, is doomed to burn in hellfire for eternity. If they knew Christ as the author does, they would be forced to change their minds. How, then, can the author possibly know such a great man if he has never accepted Christianity or any other religion?

The answer to this question lies in the fact that the truth cannot be given to those whose minds are closed. The minds of sincerely religious people *are* closed. They believe that which they are taught by men on earth and, for the majority, the doctrines are all they want to know.

The truth is not contained in any branch of Christianity, therefore the last person likely to be entrusted with the truth is a Christian.

Having maintained an open mind all his life, a person is in an ideal mental condition to receive the truth which, to the majority, is unacceptable because they just do not want to know it.

Ultimately, the truth about Jesus Christ can best be learned from the great man Himself so why is it that, of the thousands of spiritual mediums there are on earth, they never report having received a *direct* message from Christ? Christ has communicated through mediums and His words have been recorded in books.

The majority of people on earth are low spiritual beings with a minority of spiritual beings of medium spiritual height. Christ Himself is a member of the hierarchy in heaven, and High Spiritual Beings do not, other than in the most exceptional circumstances, communicate with earth people.

Jesus, having lived many times in physical bodies as we all do, is now in the highest realms in heaven where He has a heavy responsibility towards others on all the planes. This does not automatically imply that He is aloof but, because the religious population cannot be helped by Him by virtue of their totally distorted views and beliefs concerning Him, He does not attempt to interfere with their chosen patterns of life.

In other words, the greatest irony of all is that Jesus Christ is *not* interested in the Christian religion or its churches in any form. He is ashamed of the way large numbers behave in His name, even to the extent of massacring men, women and children and, in the cases of the Inquisition and the witch hunts, burning them alive by the thousand.

The priests who perpetrated such abominable crimes in the names of God and Christ have been suitably punished for being so stupid as to believe that they were granted the right, by virtue of their beliefs, to torture and kill people who chose to believe something more credible than the outrageous demands of the churches.

The barbarity of men, influenced by the stifling cloak of religion, is all the more abhorrent when they claim to worship the loving God and to be obeying God's will. To imply that God or Jesus Christ would condone such appalling behaviour against innocent people merely because they refused to accept the Christian religion is a gross insult to those Great Beings.

Contrast the behaviour of those murderous priests with a man who is, surely, the most Christ-like man to have lived on earth since Christ's disappearance, namely, Doctor Albert Schweitzer who behaved as he believed Christ would have wished him to behave. He was a minister of the church who lectured on theology and, in particular, on the life of Jesus which he studied in greater detail than anyone else had done.

It will not surprise the reader to learn that this wonderful man is now receiving his reward for his devotion to the needs of suffering humanity in Africa by virtue of the fact that he is on Plane Six in heaven and will never have to reincarnate.

At present, the Roman Catholic Church is running true to form as a totalitarian regime by virtue of the fact that a German cardinal is being arraigned before the Vatican Council to be tried for heresy. His "crime" is that he is a man who has had the temerity to think things out for himself and has come to the conclusion, correctly, that perhaps the circumstances concerning the alleged virgin birth of Christ were not substantially true.

This cardinal is doing himself a great favour spiritually by using his own innate intelligence and by challenging the rigid, unassailable beliefs of his own church. It is a great pity that more members of the clergy do not make a concerted, iconoclastic approach to the demands by the Vatican that they must believe and accept everything that they are told to believe.

This constitutes the worst kind of suppression. To tell others what they should or should not think with regard to religious matters is tantamount to mental slavery but it is a semi-voluntary slavery.

The religious masses are responsible for the perpetuation of their respective religions and it is they, and they alone, who can reduce and finally eliminate the power of the churches by thinking for themselves. Alas, the great majority of people are followers and, statistically, only one person in twenty is capable of really independent thought.

Some mediums receive messages from the departed that are tinged with, or even saturated with, religious jargon. Often, the mediums are themselves deeply religious and it is this that ensures that they can never receive the truth from heaven.

Even after death, those who were religious in life cling to their beliefs, false though they are. It is not until they reach a high plane in heaven that they finally see the futility of adhering to beliefs that are quite invalid and have no reality in the spiritual universe.

The naive concept, held by many Christians, that all the bad that they do is caused by the devil, and that all the good they do is performed by Christ or God, is a total denial of responsibility.

It is an easy way out to try to avoid liability for their own behaviour by blaming the Devil. There is no such entity as the Devil but there certainly are spiritual beings in heaven who behave in a devilish way, as do some people on earth. Every individual is responsible for his or her own behaviour. It is no good pleading with God to make you good. He cannot do that. You must work towards making yourself good because you, and you alone, create your own spiritual status.

To believe, as do millions, that membership of a church automatically ensures that they will be welcomed into the arms of Jesus when they die, is a part of the general wishful thinking that obtains throughout Christianity and is yet another delusion.

The popes, all of whom arrive on the lowest plane in heaven after death, are tragically disillusioned to discover that not only have God or Jesus Christ no desire even to meet them, but that they are on the lowest rung of the spiritual ladder. They simply cannot come to terms with the fact that, having spent a lifetime praying and indulging in all the religious ritual of their vocation, they have achieved nothing at all in spiritual terms.

Claiming, as they do, to be the custodians of the spiritual welfare of others, the clergy find after death that they have not even begun to understand what is the purpose of life or the true, spiritual nature of man.

Since one's understanding has to be raised to advance spiritually, those indoctrinated by the erroneous teachings of the churches cannot rise significantly until they have abandoned all religious beliefs.

One can understand the feelings of a pope who makes this discovery when he dies. He knows that he will have to reincarnate to try to atone for the years spent distorting the minds of the world's populations and he does not look forward to the prospect with relish.

The road to high spirituality is a long and hard one and only those people who are prepared to bring to bear the full force of their own intellect can ever make the grade.

Nowadays, there is a considerable interest, particularly among the young, in the facts of existence. Many turn to one or another religion in a vain search for the answers. Others become ascetics and isolate themselves from the rest of humanity in the forlorn hope that meditation, self-denial and a refusal to contribute to the needs of society are all the ingredients necessary to ensure them a high place in heaven.

Unfortunately for such people, they are deluding themselves. We are here on the planet earth to work, to learn and to atone and any activity or the lack of it that allows people to avoid those three things should not be condoned, otherwise they only condemn themselves to further reincarnations until they do learn how to behave.

Has belief any real value at all? Yes, but only to the extent that the belief should be restricted to the *possibility* of something being true. It is desirable that people believe that God exists, for He does. It is, however, undesirable that they should believe everything that they are told by the religions about God because not one of them on earth knows God's true nature or function in heaven.

An essential part of the Roman Catholic version of Christianity is the sanctification of certain members of the church. Those who claim to have seen visions of the "Virgin" or Christ or, perhaps, have been present during the healing of a sick person, are well on the way to being awarded the title, invariably posthumously, of saint. This is a man-made status in the same way as the position of pope is and has absolutely nothing to do with God.

There are no saints in heaven. That is to say that those so revered as such on earth are definitely not similarly regarded in heaven. Firstly, owing to their profound indoctrination with the false teachings of Christianity, they find themselves in deep doctrinal trouble after they pass on. This applies, of course, not only to the saints but to all those who have conducted their lives along the dogmatic principles of an orthodox religion.

The result of the struggle of conscience versus misunderstanding is to leave the individual utterly confused and bitterly disillusioned. This usually means that he will remain on a low plane in heaven receiving guidance and tuition from others, if he is willing to accept such help, until such time as he feels he is ready for another attempt to lead a fruitful life on earth, this time without allowing his subconscious memory of the truth that he has been taught to be wiped out and distorted by becoming involved in yet another religion.

The trite aphorisms that form part of the hypostasis of some versions of Christianity are largely responsible for the perpetuation of an erroneous concept of the spiritual existence. For example, "We are all one." We most definitely are *not* all one! We are all individuals. I should hate to think that I was one with the violent and wicked people who live on earth. "God is within us." Because God is also a created Spiritual Being, He cannot be within us. Remember, God is not our Creator.

"God is merciful." It is impossible to be impartial and merciful. There is no mercy shown by God although He is intensely compassionate. God must remain impartial otherwise He cannot fulfil His function of arranging kharmas. The Christian idea of God's mercy implies that He indulges in nepotism and that one may receive preferential consideration from Him merely by praying or asking for it.

The liturgical chanting and monotonous repetition of pleas to God for mercy and forgiveness that form part of some church services constitute a futile practice in terms of spiritual salvation. There is no mercy! Atonement is inescapable.

There is no forgiveness! Kharma is always impartially applied by God. No religious act can alter a person's kharma for the better.

If the church authorities were to spend more time studying the true spiritual existence and not their own particular brand of apologetics, they might achieve something worthwhile, yet they bicker and argue professing to seek unification of the numerous Christian churches, but often in reality wishing to adhere only to the rules of their own "club".

It should be obvious to anyone that the manifold schisms in Christianity merely emphasise its weaknesses.

A CRITIQUE OF CHRISTIANITY

The essence of Christianity, as with the majority of religions, is *belief*.   Unless one believes the dogma and the bible as interpreted in one of many diverse ways by the great number of sects, one is informed by the priests that salvation is unattainable.   Therefore, whichever Church takes the fancy of the practising Christian, the first essential is that the teachings of that particular branch of religion be accepted totally, without question and without reservation.

The second demand is that the believer shall now conform with the practical routines as laid down by the ecclesiastical hierarchy. This involves going to church at regular intervals, particularly on Sunday. While there, the congregation, en masse, are called upon to repeat prayers that they have said on every previous occasion when similarly assembled. Led by the officiating priest, they kneel in humility and submission before pleading or more frequently *ordering* God to perform certain acts for them or others, since the imperative mood is predominant in prayers.

A perfect example of the kind of prayer that has no value whatever is the so-called Lord's prayer. This does not stand up to analysis at all well. In the first place, it does not contain Christ's original words or meanings but let us examine it phrase by phrase. "Our Father which art in heaven."   God is *not* our Father but He is certainly in heaven. "Hallowed be Thy name." In effect, this is worshipful eulogy. "Thy kingdom come."   This phrase is allegorical because God does not rule as King. "Thy will be done on earth." God's will has been done before you were born and your life is up to you, for you have free will. "As it is in heaven." No one in heaven would ever consider going against God's wishes unless they were low spiritual beings but God will always have the ultimate power of reincarnating people.

Now we come to the commands typical of praying Christians who can see nothing wrong in using the imperative mood to their God. "*Give us* this day our daily bread!"   This is a direct order, not a request and is not even preceded by "please".   "And *forgive us* our trespasses!" Another command but one to which God most definitely turns a deaf ear. No trespass is ever forgiven. "As we forgive them that trespass against us." How many people *do* forgive others for the harm that they do them. Some may but others seek revenge.   "*Lead us not* into temptation!"   Another direct order but is it not impertinent to imply that God *would* ever lead people into temptation?   "But *deliver us* from evil."   As much as to say, "You, God, have the responsibility for keeping me from evil, I deny it."   "For thine is the kingdom, the power and the glory, world without end." More panegyrics.

What possible value can a prayer such as this have? In fact, it has absolutely none other than to act as padding for the church services and to contribute towards a justification of the priest's vocation.

The total denial of personal responsibility expressed by Christians ubiquitously is typical of the multitudinous examples of religious error inherent in the faith.

In the following examination of the creed, the false beliefs are in italics.

"I believe in God, *the Father Almighty, maker of heaven and earth* and in Jesus Christ, *His only Son, our Lord who was conceived by the Holy Ghost, born of the Virgin Mary,* suffered under Pontius Pilate, was crucified, dead and buried. *He descended into hell. On the third day, He rose again from the dead, He ascended into heaven and sitteth on the right hand of God the Father Almighty. From thence, He shall come to judge the quick and the dead.* I believe in the *Holy Ghost,* the *Holy* Catholic Church, *the communion of saints, the forgiveness of sins the resurrection of the body* and the life everlasting."

When the false beliefs of Christians are removed from their creed, it can be seen that the entire substance of the faith crumbles into dust.

Similarly, the responsibility for one's own behavioural improvement is firmly placed upon God in the saying of grace. "For what we are about to receive, may the Lord make us truly thankful." Why should the Lord be responsible for *making* people thankful? Have they so little empathy with their God that they cannot find it within themselves to express their thanks in a sincere way that originates in and emanates from the centre of their being?

The monotonous and repetitive chanting of prayers, sometimes half sung is, along with many other devices, one way that the priests are assured of holding the attention of their congregations, since it is a form of self-mesmerism. Can these practices really raise a person in spiritual stature? The answer is, "No!".

Hymn singing is a vital part of "worship" in all Christian churches but let us consider what worship implies. Worship is a form of adoration intended to achieve a special benefit for each individual worshipper. It is as though one is saying, "I am standing here before You, Lord, praising You, so please notice me!"

If a human being seeks to be worshipped, it is considered to be a sin and rightly so because vanity would be the predominant quality in the person concerned. How can it be right, then, to worship God? Does it not imply that He must be infinitely vain and does it not smack of attempting to inveigle one's way into God's good books?

The Genesis story in the light of scientific knowledge is ridiculously implausible. For example, it is stated that the world was created in six days but time is entirely arbitrary in universal terms. It must always remain beyond the comprehension of man as to how such creation could be possible. The priests of old were regarded by their followers as omniscient, therefore any question asked of them had to be answered. Hence the story of Genesis.

The doctrine of the Trinity is a piece of dogma, a close study of which reveals some shortcomings to say the least. "God the Father, God the Son and God the Holy Ghost". It is *assumed* that God is the Father of all mankind and this leads to the assumption that Christ was the Son of God but the assertion by some that Christ was God incarnate gives even the most agile mind a sense of paranoia. There is a strong basis for confusion about this because it is not generally known that God is not our Creator. There is proof everywhere of the existence of a Creator but God's function is the supervision of people's kharmas.

At Christ's baptism, a voice from above is reported to have said,

"Thou art my beloved son, in whom I am well pleased." Mark,1,11. It is naturally assumed that this was God's voice. In fact, it belonged to the leader of the spiritual hierarchy who had a deep concern for Christ's welfare. He was using the word "son" in a friendly sense, as a priest of today will address a young man as "my son". Alternatively, it was intended to convey to the assembled people that Christ was of such importance that He was regarded as a son by the speaker.

To infer from this biblical episode that Christ actually was the Son of God is not justifiable. If Christ *was* God then why did He frequently refer to God as His Father, He would have been talking about Himself! Also, on the occasion that Christ spoke directly to God, --- "Forgive them, Father, for they know not what they do!", He would have been talking to Himself.

I submit that no rationally-minded person can accept this. It is obvious that upon looking deeply into the various aspects of the Christian religion there are so many anomalies that the only way in which the religion could be accepted is by a blind belief, ignoring the fact that many of the tenets do not stand up to the most superficial scrutiny.

The Catholics are told by the pope that unless they take the eucharist regularly they cannot have eternal life. All life is eternal as there is no death but, no matter whether one partakes of the communion or not, life will continue after death regardless of creed.

By now, the Christians should be able to tell the world how to rise spiritually so high that they may remain in heaven for ever in a state of joy but they cannot because they do not know how. If you attend church regularly, sing hymns, say prayers and pay alms it would seem that you will, after death, walk with God in the highest realms, according to belief.

"All men (and presumably women) are born in sin", is a Christian tenet and this, in fact, comes closer to the truth than most of the remainder of the widely-held beliefs. A brief study of any of the news media will show straight away that this beautiful planet on which we exist does not conduce towards the happiness of the vast majority of its inhabitants.

All people suffer in some way at some time in their lives but does the Christian religion tell us why? No, it does not. It is believed that a newly-born child is a sinner at birth because of the so-called lapse of Eve in the Garden of Eden. What a preposterous claim! That everyone born since Eve is automatically a sinner merely because of her supposed indiscretion which forms one of the more puerile bible stories that were created by misguided priests with an axe to grind.

We suffer as a result of our sins, it is claimed. Oh, yes! Most definitely we do. What about the newly-born babe, though? If it is a newly-created soul, in accordance with Christian teaching, then how could it have incurred such congenital punishments as blindness, deafness, autism, spasticity, spina bifida, leukaemia and so on, as do large numbers of babies?

This would seem to be a terrible injustice especially if, as Christians believe, it is God's will. The God of Love, then, creates these pathetic children because of Eve's mistaken waywardness. Or does He?

There is only one answer to the enigma of human suffering. If there is any kind of justice on earth or in heaven at all, then each individual sufferer *must* have deserved such punishment and the only possible way that a newly born child could have incurred such a penalty as blindness, for example, is for that child to have lived before during which life or lives the behaviour of the person was such as to result in the apparently terrible burden of loss of sight. Why "apparently?", you may ask. Because, if you really knew what crimes or sins were perpetrated by the blind baby in an earlier life in a different physical body, then you might well think that it was being let off lightly.

Few Christians, though, will accept reincarnation and, to the Catholics, it is heresy. All reference to it by Christ was removed from the bible centuries ago because it did not suit the priests to leave it in. Remember that men wrote the bible and not God. Men decided what to leave in or to take out of the scriptures for religious or, frequently, political reasons.

Let us now compare belief with Truth. "God is omnipotent." False. God is extremely powerful and has an unimaginably onerous responsibility towards all incarnate beings but He cannot do everything.

"God the Father." False. Not only is God not the father of Christ, He is not the father of mankind either collectively or individually.

"God the Creator." False. God did not create the universe or the spiritual beings or physical bodies in it. The Creator is a separate Being.

"God the Holy Ghost." This is merely religious jargon.

"God's blessing." It will come as a disappointment to millions to learn that there is no such thing. You reap as you have sown. If your fortunes are in the ascendancy, you can be sure you have earned this "blessing". If they are not, then you have similarly deserved your condition.

"God's will". After they have been incarnated, God does not attempt to exert His will on people. They are on their own and, within the constraints imposed upon them by society and their fellow men, they have free will. It *is* God's will that people shall atone for their crimes by successive incarnations ultimately to remain in heaven in a very high spiritual state where they continue to help and serve others but this will is impressed upon the spiritual being's subconscious mind at the moment of incarnation. God most certainly exists but He is a very different Being from the image of Him that has been created by the Christians.

The truth is so different from the beliefs of people that it is not surprising that few can accept it even when it is offered to them.

In order to satisfy the demands and answer the questions of their devotees, the priests of old realised that they had to give the impression that they knew all the answers to the basic questions of life. When asked who created the earth and every being on it they, not unnaturally, claimed that God was responsible. The result was the story in Genesis concerning the creation of the world and man.

Having assumed that God was responsible for everything, the churchmen then created an image of Him as omnipotent, omniscient, omnipresent, the giver of all life, the pardoner of sins and the controller of human behaviour. This typical concept of God is far from accurate and the only truth contained here is that God's mind is omnipresent.

God is not all-powerful although he can bring to bear enormous influence. Even He cannot turn water into wine and neither, incidentally, could Christ.

In the many scripts that Amanda and I have taken and the conversations that we have had with God, He has explained His attributes that I am now describing, stressing that He is not our Creator. God has told us that He does not know everything in the universe but that His knowledge is very encompassing and far-reaching. He would not, for example, know all the theory and practice of computer technology. He can call upon numerous experts in every field of human activity and this He does, when necessary.

In His spiritual body, God can only be in one place at a time either in the spiritual or physical universe or both together. There is one tremendous difference between God's mind and that of all other spiritual beings. His awareness can be directed to anywhere in the universe and to an infinite number of places simultaneously. This explains how it is that God can receive prayers from millions of people at once.

Neither the earth nor the universe was created by God. He has a vital function and a unique one in heaven. It is He who examines our records throughout our many incarnations and it is He who decides how and when we shall atone by further lives in physical bodies or when we have reached a spiritual status high enough to render a further incarnation unnecessary.

Life forms were not originated by God but He ensures their continuity by supervising the genetic developmental progress of animal and human forms. Thus, He is able to reincarnate a spiritual being into a spastic body or to inflict as an atonement any of the countless adverse conditions of the human physical entity.

The propagation of species by sexual activity is a self-perpetuating process that is not directly under God's control, but He can direct that certain spiritual beings shall be born into certain families, ethnic societies and so on.

Once a conception has occurred, unless a spiritual being is introduced into the developing foetus, the infant will be mis-carried or still-born.

No sins are ever forgiven, so the percept of God as the merciful, forgiving Being is fallacious. Benign, He most certainly is, but He cannot take pity on anyone, or pardon them for their misbehaviour, as He has to act in a totally impartial manner. In this way, everyone has free choice to determine their own spiritual evolution.

If people could merely ask for forgiveness and receive it, how facile an evasion of personal responsibility that would be!

Every human being incarnate has the freedom to determine his own behaviour. God does *not* influence or control people after they have been incarnated except in the rarest of circumstances.

Living and working on the highest plane in heaven, God is in constant communication with High Spiritual Beings who are not angels or saints since these words are not used in heaven. The ultimate in spiritual height can only be achieved after the individual spiritual entity has endured many lives in physical bodies of many different types and at the same time learnt lessons while contributing to the welfare of individuals, groups, nations or mankind as a whole.

Good behaviour is rewarded by an associated rise in spiritual height. Bad behaviour is negative to the extent that one remains at the same low level or even regresses, spiritually.

Those who harbour negative attitudes such as jealousy, hatred, envy, greed, selfishness and resentment only harm themselves and cannot rise up the spiritual ladder. In contrast, those who put others first and foster the more positive aspects of human nature such as selfless love, compassion, altruism, responsibility as a member of society, generosity and good humour will, during each lifetime, gain considerably in spiritual height.

The aims of the Christians appear to be to attain the highest states of existence and receive their rewards in heaven. This is entirely praiseworthy but, while their motives may be genuine enough, the methods that they use in attempting to achieve their goals are not only highly suspect but downright false and, in terms of actual gain, are a complete waste of valuable life time.

How does one go about telling a priest that he is wasting his life? For most, it is a living, for others, a vocation; for yet others, a devotion. Those who have built themselves an ivory tower of Christianity are hardly likely to throw themselves from the top or attempt to tear it down but, after their re-entry into heaven after "death", they have to start learning, all over again, the truth about God and Christ.

This truth is in such contrast with the so-called truth taught by the churches that, for most, it is a great uphill struggle to accept it. It is a sad fact that those whose religious fervour in life is the deepest find themselves on the lowest planes in heaven after their passing and then spend, maybe, many centuries essaying to rid themselves of the erroneous teachings of Christianity. They find that there are millions of spiritual beings, spiritually higher than they are, who were not in the least religious in their last lives even to the point of being atheistic.

It is far better to be an atheist and to lead a good life than to be religious and do the same thing. This may sound ridiculous, at first, but a significant factor in individual spiritual evolution is *understanding*. Whereas neither understands the reasons for his existence and misfortunes, at least the atheist returns to heaven with a mind undistorted by the totally misleading preachings of religion.

On the other hand, the zealot returns to heaven in great expectation and is grossly disappointed to discover, as do the highly-placed Christian prelates, that they have spent a whole lifetime in the service of the church only to be back at the bottom rung of the ladder again. The reason that they find themselves in such an odious position is that their real level of understanding is very, very low.

The atheist's mind is, at least, still unfettered by dogma and he is usually, unless self-opinionated and obdurate, mentally free to learn the truth.

Imagine, if you can, the feelings of a person who has believed all his life that Christ died on the cross for his sins and that devotion to Christ in church would ensure his salvation when, after death, he

63

learns that Christ did *not* die on the cross. Therefore, the whole basis of his belief is undermined. Further, to believe that one man can, by his own suffering and death, atone for the sins of others is wishful thinking. It is comparable with the sacrifice of one person in a group to a lion so that the rest may escape. It was not like that. It *is* not like that.

No person on earth has ever been able, or will ever be able, to atone for the sins of others. You must atone for your own crimes. It is the only path to the final release from successive incarnations.

Priests who claim to be able to grant people absolution from their sins are deluded. No person on earth is in a position to absolve another from that other's crimes. Surely, this should be evident without indulging in deep thought but millions believe that they can commit a crime on Saturday, confess it to a priest on Sunday and have it wiped from their slate. No! They can not. It simply is impossible. No amount of church-going, hymn singing or praying will enable a person to absolve himself from a sin or crime, neither will the practice of penances imposed by a priest.

There exist only two basic ways of atoning for sin. One is by suffering to the extent that you have caused others to suffer, and the other is by balancing out the evil that you have done by countering it with good behaviour. What part can the church play in this?

Absolution, as part of Christian teaching, is a myth. Genuflection and prostration as practised in nunneries represent forms of self-humiliation that border on the masochistic. None of the similar ritual devices, such as crossing oneself, can possibly influence one's destiny. Why do people allow themselves to become part of the pointless ceremonial conduct insisted upon by the churches?

Many people are content to let others do their thinking for them, so, rather than bring to bear their own analytical powers on the subjects of existence and survival after death, they submit to almost any implausible dogma and soak up the hypnotic, repetitious creed of the church until they become religious automata.

Egged on by family pressure and by the threats of priests concerning the dire penalties of failing to attend church or failing to pay alms to the church, they become fearful and, from then on, they are in a trap that they have entered of their own volition.

Considerable numbers of children are forced into the Christian churches' way of thinking. The fortunate few, able to extricate themselves from the web of false ideas, tenets and dogmas through the exercise of their intellects are, sometimes, able to see the insidious nature of religious training and escape from the mental cage which they instinctively are aware is inhibiting their spiritual growth.

Those who decide to spend their entire adult lives in monasteries or nunneries in order, as they obviously sincerely believe, to serve God, are doing the exact opposite. In what way do they think they are helping God? Perhaps by praying.

For a moment, let us consider the subject of prayer. Prayers are received only by God and not by the saints who are created by priests nor by any other spiritual being in heaven. Christ does not answer prayers. If the supplicant has a sufficiently good record to warrant the granting of a fervent wish expressed in prayer, then God may arrange, through one or more of His countless servants in heaven that the wish be granted.

If the prayer is for one's own, or another's improved health or recovery from illness then it will only be answered if the person prayed for has deserved it. God does answer individual prayers but only when the person's past behaviour justifies such action.

Mass prayer, though, can achieve nothing because a community or nation is composed of individuals who are all different and have had different past lives and experiences, each with a unique kharma.

The constant, monotonous chanting and singing of prayers in churches, monasteries or nunneries achieve nothing and are a sheer waste of time. This does *not* serve God. God is best served by each individual leading his own life according to his instincts and inclinations in the workaday world and not by self-incarceration within a prison-like monastic establishment, there to rise in the middle of the night to intone ritual prayers that are pointless and to deny himself, in some extreme cases, even the most important need of all people, namely, communication with one's fellows, as in the silent orders.

Self-abnegation, as a form of atonement, achieves nothing. As a means of self-discipline, however, it has merit inasmuch as it acts as a brake upon one's desires to indulge excessively in the material pleasures of life.

Fasting is yet another ploy connived at by the priests of old in order to maintain an apparency of superiority over their flocks. The analogy between sheep and people in the context of religion is often appropriate since both follow the leader without thought.

Certainly, there are priests who, having survived their theological college studies, have grave misgivings concerning the teachings of the church. Not a few expect to discover the reasons for their existence and what will happen to them after death but, in their advanced years, they become disillusioned. This is not surprising as, after a lifetime of praying for people's recovery from illness and seldom seeing any results, their doubts are strengthened. Then, as their own lives approach the end on earth and people ask them what it is like to die and what happens after death, the priests just do not know.

The irony of this situation is apparent. Supposedly nurturing the spiritual development of their congregations as a vocation and being paid for it, the teachers of the Christian faith find themselves none the wiser when it comes to the basic questions of life and death.

The priest may only express in public the orthodox religious views, no matter what his actual knowledge may be, otherwise he risks excommunication. Such is the snare of religion that the intelligent, well-educated, altruistic man is, by allowing his mind to be influenced by the concrete, deeply-entrenched thoughts of an almost infinite line of priests before him, denying his own priceless, individual ability to discern fact from fiction and right from wrong.

It is a crime in itself to subordinate one's natural perspicacity to the engulfing, cloying cobwebs of preconceived thought.

Lest the reader should imagine that this is a diatribe against Christ, it should be understood that Christ is a wonderful and remarkable man. Yes, a man, not a god. He was reincarnated from Plane Five after volunteering in heaven where He had completed His spiritual evolution in physical bodies, having lived eleven previous lives.

Sent to earth by the hierarchy in heaven and not by God, Jesus knew that He had a vital job to do. That job was to bring enlightenment to the materialistic peoples of the time, amongst whom were the most barbaric and callously indifferent human beings.

Enlightenment, in the spiritual sense, consists of explaining the true, eternal, spiritual nature of man and all biological forms and expounding upon the behaviour necessary to enable each individual to achieve high spiritual status. Jesus Christ tried to do this against formidable opposition, ridicule and overt hostility.

The enormity of His task can hardly be comprehended by the average person but the outstandingly significant factor in His purpose is that He was never intended to become the subject of a religion. Men have taken the life of Christ as an example of selfless devotion and unlimited love for His fellow men, which it was indeed, but then they attempted to apotheosise Him.

By leaving out of the bible those sayings of Christ that they could not understand and by falsifying where they thought it necessary in order to fit their preconceived ideas as to what the Messiah should be, the priests ruined most of Christ's work.

Ever since His disappearance after the crucifixion, Jesus has been the victim of misrepresentation and deification. His mission was, basically, simple but to put it into effect proved to be impossible owing to the crass ignorance and spiritual blindness of the people. This, combined with the numerous false beliefs spread about Him and the bible mistranslations, deletions, omissions and alterations, contributed towards the creation by the Christians of a man who has never existed.

The English versions of the bible were translated from the original Aramaic into Hebrew, from Hebrew into Greek and from Greek into Latin and English, since when, theologians have altered the text to suit their own interpretations and have also modified the language.

The various versions of the bible in different languages frequently differ in the use of words indicating, yet again, that the bible, in many respects, bears little resemblance to the original documents.

The stories concerning Jesus Christ were written down many years after the events occurred and were often elaborated so as to fit in with the already existing prophecies.

Jesus Christ's disciple, Peter, reached Rome in 42 A.D. and wrote the epistle to the Romans. Then, Paul arrived in Rome between 59 and 61 A.D. and the Acts, Mark, Luke and Peter were written.

A convocation of priests was held in about the year 268 A.D. during the reign of Gallienus, 260 to 270 A.D., who issued an edict of toleration for the Christians and restored them the use of their churches. After a further forty years, a very strange Christian intellectual appeared in the East. He was Paul of Samosata, bishop of Antioch, an ambitious and powerful prelate and was the author of a new kind of theology. Paul was deposed from office at the convocation of 268 A.D. and was succeeded by Domnus. It was perfectly obvious that the church and politics went hand in hand.

Paul was saluted with honorific chants and liturgies on entering church and he could be politician, business-man, orator, philosopher or theologian. Female ministers were in the church, then, and were known as deaconesses. Today, women are struggling to be re-admitted as priestesses.

The Essenes were a pre-Christian order of Jewish monks. The name means "King Bees". They are not mentioned in the bible but their mode of life has been described by Jewish, Christian and pagan writers. At one time, over four thousand of them lived in agricultural settlements and they constituted a league of virtue.

The Essene Order were a strict novitiate. They indulged in semi-ascetic practices and silent meals. They wore white robes, and baths and prayers were all part of their routine. They appeared and disappeared in an aura of mystery, leaving barely a clue to their existence. None of their sacred books has survived.

There were two Orders of Essenes, one of which allowed marriage in order to perpetuate the race, the other did not. Right living was instilled into both Orders to the extent that they paid little heed to the material needs of man but they were taught piety, justice, citizenship and how to discern right from wrong. They did not swear or tell lies and they exercised self-control, endurance, simplicity, good humour, modesty, regard for the law and fitness of character.

As their mode of life was so strict yet so honourable, it was decided by the Gardeners of the Earth that this was the most suitable Order for Jesus Christ to join so that He could have the very specialised training needed for Him to accomplish the task that He was intended to do.

Jesus Christ existed all right but He was not born of a virgin. His conception and birth were normal and He was the third child of Mary.

Extraordinary circumstances attended Christ's birth by virtue of the so-called Star of Bethlehem which was not a star but a spaceship.

In the bible, it states "- and, lo, the star, which they saw in the east, went before them, till it came and stood over where the young child was". Matthew, chapter 2, verse 9. Obviously, a star cannot behave in such a manner but a space craft can and did. Throughout the bible there are references to voices from on high, brightly illuminated objects and people suspended above the ground.

The interest in Christ's mission, initiated by the heavenly hierarchy, continued throughout His life and He was in frequent communication with the highest spiritual beings in heaven but seldom directly with God.

When those aspects of biblical writings that baffle the clergy are clarified, it becomes obvious that the appearances and influences most remarked upon were *not* those of God.

Where the plain truth *is* stated in the bible, it is invariably mis-interpreted by the priests. For example, Ezekiel's visions in the first chapter of his book were actual events described by him in the only language available to him. The events were so startling and the objects that he saw were so unfamiliar that his basic terminology was unable to convey precisely what he was seeing. The priests who came later and read Ezekiel's writings could not begin to understand what he was describing so they decided that he was "seeing things", in other words, experiencing a psychic vision.

A modern-day example of the meddling that has gone on for centuries with the bible is that, in a recent, "modernised" version, Ezekiel's wonderful description of a spaceship and its occupants (Ezekiel, Chap.1) has been altered so that the beings flying around are now called animals. Those responsible for the wording in this version of the bible are also guilty of distorting still further the original statements so that the truth has become more remote than ever.

Ezekiel, chapter 40, verse 2 in the King James version of the bible states, "In the visions of God brought he me into the land of Israel", but, in the new version this reads, "In a vision God brought me to the land of Israel". This has an entirely different meaning and is *not* what Ezekiel meant. "In the visions of God" meant that Ezekiel was seeing the same things as the Being he referred to as God was seeing.

It was, in fact, the Lord God who made frequent appearances in His spiritual spaceship who was reported many times. The same Lord God continues to appear to people on earth and has been seen by numerous observers.

These examples illustrate the paucity of understanding of the theologians entrusted with the perpetuation of the bible. In order to arrive at a good understanding of the contents of the bible, it is necessary to relinquish all remnants of religious convictions and to study the available evidence, with all its faults and errors, with a critical, unbiased eye. As soon as one drops the conviction that Christ was superhuman, it begins to become clear that He *was* human but able to make far more use of His natural talents because of the great assistance that He continually received from the spiritual world, or heaven.

Those who understand the true nature of the spirit are better able to be effective in life, especially when it comes to assisting others with their physical and mental ailments, emotional problems and every day troubles.

Christ's healing abilities are well-documented and He knew that the healing power did not come *from* Him but *through* Him. Once the religious leaders had decided that Jesus was the promised saviour, they had to fit Him into the pattern predicted by the prophets. They tried to do this but they only ended up by completely falsifying Him, His statements and His work.

Owing to the limited vocabulary of the average person who listened to Jesus, He found it necessary to resort to the parable in order to put across His meaning. If He were to have spoken in direct terms, the listeners would neither have believed Him nor understood Him.

The same situation exists here on earth nearly two thousand years later. People would rather believe than know. Somehow, they feel secure in their faith, wrong as it is. When confronted with the truth, many reject it out of hand, partly because of fear that they may, after all, have been responsible for their own fates and partly because it is so vastly different from the teachings of Christianity.

To attempt to emulate Christ's loving and helpful approach to people is highly commendable and it can, in fact, be practised by anyone whether religious or otherwise but it is *not* necessary to belong to a church in order to do that.

To claim, as do most churches, that only membership of their particular church will guarantee you a high place in heaven is taking religion too far. What it amounts to is that those who know the least about existence make the most preposterous claims about it.

Let us just consider one of the more extreme aspects of religions. These are the sects that, every few years, predict the end of the world by flood, so they all climb a mountain to await the inundation in the firm belief that God has chosen them, alone, to survive. After a night or two camping out they, rather sheepishly, return to their homes. The fact that the expected event never happens does not seem to strike them as odd and appears not to shake their faith in their particular brand of religion or its leaders.

One of the prime characteristics necessary to devote oneself to the Christian religion, as opposed to adopting Christ's characteristics as one's own, is gullibility. Of course, many children all over the world are in the trap the moment they are born. The religion is instilled into them as soon as they can speak and understand. The rituals and the religious calendar are adhered to, the children are forced to be present in church whether their instinct tells them it is wrong or not and, finally, they are totally indoctrinated and, from then on, unable to think any further for themselves on the subject.

The converted are prepared to place infinite faith in their priests who, in many cases, are quite unsuited to act as advisors in spite of being well-meaning.

The principle of allowing celibate priests to pontificate upon birth control and sexual problems is one of the more bizarre aspects of Catholicism.

The obduracy of the popes concerning artificial means of birth control is responsible for much of the misery in the world, resulting as it does in unwanted children, often by poverty-stricken families, thus raising the populations of some areas to a point where the economy cannot support them. Then, they starve.

On analysis, the consumption of bread and wine in the belief that they represent the body and blood of Christ, even though symbolically, is a cannibalistic ritual. Is it necessary to go to such lengths in order to attain salvation? No, it is not, but because of Christ's reported words at the Last Supper, this particular ritual is considered vital.

Salvation can be achieved only by the efforts of the individual, with guidance from others where necessary but it cannot be achieved by any religious ritual participated in by man.

The millions of practising Catholics are, without being aware of it, allowing themselves to be used by the perpetuators of a totalitarian religion the tenets of which and whose creeds are almost entirely fallacious.

Those who have endured a lifetime of religious suppression, upon arrival in heaven after death of the body, are bitterly disillusioned to discover that, had they left religion strictly alone, they would, almost invariably, be spiritually higher. They are then able to see things more clearly and the sight of a devoted ex-nun or ex-monk in heaven who has come to the realisation that their last incarnation was almost in vain is pitiful to behold.

"Believe and ye shall be saved!" state the sandwich boards. Unfortunately, much more than mere belief is needed in order for any one to be "saved". What does this mean? Saved from what?

You can save yourself from further atonement, which usually means more incarnations, by behaving only as previously described. It is always up to the individual to achieve his own spiritual advancement. Some want to but cannot. Many do not want to. Others achieve considerable spiritual gains during a lifetime, entirely without adherence to any particular creed, merely by behaving in a decent, civilised and considerate manner to all those with whom they come into contact. Upon arrival in heaven again, they are in an infinitely better position than those who have run their lives around a religion as a devotion. It has frequently been observed that there are more Christian people outside religion than there are in it. When one observes the behaviour of some people with closed minds it is not surprising. To some, the purchase of a pew in church in order to set them apart from, and above the others, is more important than the spiritual values.

There are those who use their church as a kind of social club and go to pick up the latest gossip. Yet others go because they feel that it is expected of them and not on account of religious leanings.

Highly-placed politicians and, of course, royalty, patronise the church because it represents an historical precedent and it is expected of them. The British monarch is still regarded as the defender of the faith. The pageantry of royal church ceremonies forms a colourful focal point for the nation.

In summary, then, the actual practising of religion cannot raise a person spiritually, therefore it fails completely in its very purpose. That which church members do to help each other and others is a different matter. All good deeds, whether in the name of religion or not, result in rewards to the individuals who carry them out.

Missionaries who bring material benefits to suppressed and under-privileged peoples do wonderful work and often their lives are at risk but the moment they start to convert those people to Christianity they do great harm. Admittedly, the missionaries are courageous, devoted and selfless people with a genuine desire to help humanity and for that they are rewarded. For converting a tribe with a simple religious faith to Christianity, which has the effect of confusing many of them, the missionaries will receive no reward because they are stunting the spiritual development of the people as their own is already stunted.

The question may be asked, "Why do millions of people join the sects, cults and churches of Christianity?" In the first place, while they are in heaven between incarnations, they are aware that God is a prominent and active High Spiritual Being whose word is law.

Secondly, after being re-born, there is a sub-conscious memory of God in the minds of millions and this leads them to accept a religion that preaches that God is almighty. As all the religions on earth preach false data they are extremely disappointed to learn, upon their re-arrival in heaven at death, that the hours, days, weeks, months and years spent in church were not only a waste of their precious lifetime but were, in fact, responsible in the majority of cases, for their spiritual retrogression.

The ephemeral euphoria enjoyed by many devotees of some of the fringe cults is but a soporific. The multitudes appear to need religion as much as they need food and, if they were prevented from indulging their craving and given no alternative many of them would become emotionally the worse. Their simple faith is, to millions, often their only palliative in a hostile world and, lacking intellectual insight, they lean heavily upon the crutch of their church.

The confessional can be highly therapeutic because the priest may often be the only person in whom the individual may feel disposed to confide but the benefits to him are limited to a feeling of relief at having rid himself of a burden of grief, guilt or remorse. The priest who believes that he can absolve another person's sins is labouring under a delusion. He cannot recognise that when Christ said, "For whatsoever a man soweth, that shall he also reap", He meant it!

The spiritual status of the individual is not determined by the number of times one goes to church nor by the number of sins confessed.

Within the Christian movement, there exist organisations whose raison d'être and whose deeds represent the highest moral conduct. Such groups may contain dedicated, courageous and self-less people who in order to bring succour to others in need frequently expose themselves to great risk and, sometimes, to the loss of their own lives. These people are, by their good works, working out their own kharmas and raising themselves spiritually. It is important to realise that their practical, altruistic approach to mankind is *their* salvation and not the ritual and routine of their church services.

One may argue that, without the Christian principles having been instilled into them, they might never have become involved in such helpful enterprises but the principles of right living are available to all and are not the sole prerogative of the churches whose past history reveals that the greatest atrocities of all time were committed by Christians, even to the extent of genocide. Their example to the world was the antithesis of Christ's teaching and in the smug, self-complacent manner of quidnuncs, they tortured, burned, destroyed, murdered and massacred thereby choosing to ignore the decalogue and to assume the mantle of God Himself by determining the fate of those whose intelligence and spiritual understanding far exceeded their own.

The crass ignorance, blind stupidity and moral torpitude of priests who could create such havoc and suffering to men, women and children are almost beyond belief. That they wrought their crimes in God's name only compounds their guilt.

There is but one consoling factor that arises out of a consideration of the cruelty of self-righteous clergy and that is the certain knowledge that every one of them will have had to suffer to the extent that he made others suffer. This is the only justice and it is not imposed by God, merely put into effect by Him.

Each of us creates his own nemesis for we *have* free will. To assume that God would raise His hand against one's enemy, merely because that enemy thought differently and held opposing beliefs, is to imply that God is not impartial and, simultaneously, to imprecate an act of evil from the God of Love.

The shallowness of understanding acquired after a life-time's study of religion has been publicly exemplified by a professor of religious studies, the sum total of whose knowledge of the spiritual existence was shown to be nought. The best that the erudite professor could do to appraise people of the life to come was to state that he believes in "some continuity of life after death, with God."

Is this all that one can learn from an academic study of religions? If so, there is something badly lacking. After a life-time of religious devotion and study, the cleric might, if he is fortunate, have

71

aspired to the realisation that there is, possibly, something after death. The nature of that something is completely incomprehensible to him, though, because his *belief* is paramount and his *knowledge* of the subject is nil.

Why do intelligent people tolerate "experts" in the field of religion who repeatedly display their lack of gnosis? Is it the fact that, as this same professor said, devotion, prayer and worship are considered the most important activities in life if salvation and eternal life are to be achieved?

The supremely important aspect of existence is the spiritual life as, without it, there is nothing. The ultimate in spiritual joy can be experienced only while discarnate, in heaven, on the highest planes.

When God examines a person's kharma, He sees the total existence, not just one's last or current incarnation. A deep understanding of the spiritual existence leads the searcher to a position where he is able to survey it as a whole. From this elevated vantage point, it is possible to assume entirely different attitudes towards the subjects that seem so vital to the peoples of earth today such as abortion, capital punishment, individual responsibility, birth control, euthanasia, sterilisation of the sexes, murder and suicide.

When the long-term effects of such acts become obvious, it is discovered that the great majority of people think wrongly about them. This is because they cannot compute into a future about which they know nothing. Knowledge is an essential prerequisite to the dispensation of wisdom but it must be *true* knowledge and not an accumulation of false ideas borrowed from ancient writings or the observations of aberrated priests of one or another of the four thousand religions extant at present.

The Truth is finally available but how many will be able to accept it? Millions will simply not comprehend and will prefer to adhere to their faith regardless of any other consideration. Theirs will be the loss.

Time after time, every day, evidence of the reality of the spiritual universe is being brought before earth's inhabitants. Alas, the learned scientists, in general, claim that eye witnesses to occult phenomena are either hallucinating or are in need of psychiatric treatment.

In the nineteenth century, the scientists began to take over from the priests the responsibility for exegesis. They believed that everything on earth could be explained by science but then they found that the more deeply they probed into matter and biological forms, the more remote the vital answers became.

Scientists have achieved amazing feats such as the discovery of DNA, deoxyribonucleic acid, which contains the programme in computerised form for the genetic development of biological species. The more deeply they probe into this the more perplexed some of them become as they expect to unravel the secret of life by peering down microscopes. They will never do this because the physical universe is a materialised replication of the spiritual universe and not vice versa.

THE CAUSE IS SPIRIT!

* * * * * * * * * * * * *

CHAPTER TEN

THE ESSENCE OF LIFE

The Basic Secrets of Existence

1   You are a spiritual being.

2   You have existed for an immense time.

3   You are immortal.

4   You have been incarnate before your
    present life.

5   You live many lives in different bodies
    which may be of any biological form and
    of either sex or any human race.

6   You are on earth now either to learn
    vital lessons or because you have
    kharma outstanding.

7   You reincarnate, repeatedly, until your
    atonement for past crimes is complete and
    you have cleared your kharma.

8   There is no death.

9   The practice of a religion *cannot* raise
    you spiritually.

* * * * * * * * * * * * *

```
*   *   *   *   *   *   *   *   *   *   *   *
```

10   No sin is ever forgiven. It must be atoned
     for. There is *no* way of avoiding atonement.

11   You, alone, are responsible for your own
     behaviour at *all* times regardless of any
     other consideration.

12   There is no such condition as diminished
     responsibility.

13   You reap as you sow. Each good deed is
     rewarded. Each bad deed is atoned for.

14   Everything that you have ever said and
     done in your total physical existence
     of many lives is recorded in heaven in
     the Akashic Record.

15   There is only one heaven.

16   There is only one punishment planet in
     the universe and that is earth. Earth is
     the only hell.

17   You have free will.

18   No birth is an accident. All births are
     according to kharma.

```
*   *   *   *   *   *   *   *   *   *   *   *
```

```
*  *  *  *  *  *  *  *  *  *  *  *
*                                        *
*    19   Suicide ends nothing. It merely ensures a      *
*         prompt reincarnation.                          *
*                                        *
*    20   God and the Creator are distinctly separate   *
*         Beings.                                        *
*                                        *
*                                        *
*  *  *  *  *  *  *  *  *  *  *  *
```

CHAPTER ELEVEN

THE PRINCIPLES OF ASTRAL TRAVELLING

The reader is warned that astral travelling is not a subject for idle experimentation and that it is essential to acquire a facility in communication with, and a deep understanding of, the spiritual world particularly with those on the higher planes, before even contemplating it. It is easy for the uninitiated to be fooled by low spiritual beings therefore the inhabitants of Planes One and Two should never be trusted to take a person astral travelling.

Since, normally, no incarnate spiritual being can travel higher than Plane Four, astral travelling means visiting, while out of the physical body, Planes One to Four of the spiritual universe but, because the physical universe may be observed from the spiritual universe, it is also possible to view any object or location in the physical universe.

Physical matter is no barrier to the spiritual body, therefore one can view the earth from any viewpoint such as under the sea or deep under the ground. The spiritual body, while astral travelling, can pass through doors, ceilings, walls and anything physical that would normally be impassable to the physical body.

Any planet in the universe may be visited and its inhabitants, if any, studied. Practically every incarnate person astral travels while asleep but because of the similarity of the spiritual planes to earth, they usually do not realise where they have been and, if they remember the experience upon waking, they think they were dreaming.

During the lifetime of a human being, the spiritual and physical bodies are united by a silver cord. At death, the spiritual mind and body return whence they came, to the spiritual universe. This process simulates physical birth and the cutting of the umbilical cord but the silver cord is severed instead and death is merely a rebirth back to the spiritual world. The only true definition of death is the severance of the silver cord that releases the spiritual being from the physical body.

After death, the mind is still intact because it is spiritual and not physical. Memory is stored in the mind and not the brain and the personality immediately after death is the same as it was immediately before it with the same memories, foibles and characteristics.

It can now be seen that the sensory centre of a human being is the mind and not the brain. All the so-called physical senses of sight, touch, taste, hearing and smell are registered by the mind for, without the mind, nothing can be experienced either in the physical or spiritual worlds.

The spiritual mind and spiritual body are inseparable but they are, together, separable from the physical body and when this occurs temporarily it is known as astral travelling. Sometimes, it is referred to as an out-of-body experience or OBE and sometimes as exteriorisation. When the separation includes the severing of the silver cord, this is known as death.

Because, in the spiritual universe the creation of an effect is achieved by a thought process, travel is achieved merely by postulating the wish to be somewhere else and one is instantaneously there.

Adverbs of time are really superfluous when describing the astral existence because there is no time but, for clarification and comparison with the physical world, I shall continue to use them.

If a person in the astral wishes to he can soar as though in a glider over the heavenly countryside or the surface of the earth.

Spiritual beings feel solid to themselves and each other but, whereas they can pass easily through any physical object, they cannot pass through each other.

All spiritual beings have a spiritual robe the colours of which denote their spiritual status but they may wear anything they choose and so, by mentally creating their clothing, it becomes a reality. Thus it is that the famous High Spiritual Beings continue to wear the style of clothing that they wore during their last lives, thereby rendering themselves instantly recognisable to others.

Some prefer to wear nothing but nudity is not regarded in heaven as a topic for rude jokes as it is on earth.

Beginners in astral travelling are invariably nude on leaving their physical bodies but, while being guided under controlled conditions, a robe is given them so that they do not appear too incongruous.

Objects that are mentally created in the astral become as solid to the creator of them and to other observers as the equivalent object would be on earth.

Astral travelling can occur in several different ways. The first is during sleep when most people travel but only the initiated would realise, upon waking, that they had actually been travelling in the astral. The majority would either think they had been dreaming or recall nothing at all.

The second type of exteriorisation occurs during moments of shock, physical or mental, and is inadvertent. Patients undergoing surgery frequently recall, after the operation, that they had been out of their bodies and can describe the operation and the physical surroundings.

Yet other patients under operation whose hearts have stopped and been restarted have experienced having visited the astral planes and have often been disappointed on being sent back to their bodies. The similarities in the descriptions of different patients are extremely significant as they constitute confirmatory evidence.

The third type of exteriorisation is achieved by a solo conscious effort. Only the courageous and those with a good understanding should normally attempt this method. Individual people have their own ways of leaving their bodies and certain techniques are described in various books by practitioners of the art. The results are very varied in these cases because few people understand what is happening or what to expect. This can result in random excursions into the astral.

The fourth type of exteriorisation occurs when an incarnate person exteriorises another by commands and guidance. This method can be extremely effective if limited to travelling in the physical universe but it is not recommended to attempt this technique to explore the astral world.

The fifth type of exteriorisation is achieved under the complete control and guidance of spiritual beings. In this case, the spiritual beings, usually two, lift the spiritual body from the physical body while the person is fully conscious and willing to be taken. Then, the

newly released spiritual being is taken first of all on a short
reconnaissance trip around the local physical environment in order to
give him experience and to acclimatise him to his new adventure.

When the tyro has realised that he can still see while out of his
body and can also move around, he is taken farther afield either into
the astral planes or to a location in the physical universe. Each
guide holds one hand of the student which gives the latter a reference
point and, therefore, confidence.

What is the beginner likely to see during his first controlled
astral travel? If he has had religious training and is still
influenced by it, either consciously or subconsciously, he will see
that which he expects to see because he mentally creates the object of
his own interest. Thus, a Christian may see cherubs which exist only
because he created them, have no basis in reality and constitute a
subjective image. Also, the Christian may misinterpret that which he
sees in the astral. For example, any High Spiritual Being that he sees
he will assume is Jesus Christ because of the brilliant aura
surrounding Him.

A High Spiritual Being does not have to belong to the hierarchy in
heaven but could be an ordinary person in a very advanced stage of
spiritual evolution. The inhabitants of Plane Five and above are known
as High Spiritual Beings.

The aspirant whose mind is not pre-conditioned by religion or an
acceptance of scientific, psychological or psychiatric teachings will
have no difficulties in astral travelling under guidance. He will see
that which is there to be seen and will have a strong reality upon it.
The sceptic, however, will usually see only darkness because he
expects nothing else.

Let us now embark upon a typical astral travel. The instructor
assumes the role of Relay whose function is, by communicating, to pass
on instructions and information from the two guides, one of whom
should always be a High Spiritual Being.

The person is, preferably, asked to lie down and close his eyes
because complete relaxation of the body is essential. Then, he is
asked to commence deep breathing until he is fully relaxed and to say
when he is ready.

The High Spiritual Being who is the leading Guide will then say to
the person via the Relay, "We are lifting you out of your body, now."
The tyro may actually experience a sensation of rising but some do
not, at first. While standing in his spiritual body behind his
physical head, the person is asked to look at his body lying on the
bed. Some see it, some do not. The same applies to the silver cord.
The astral traveller is asked to look around the room and at various
people including the Guides and other spiritual beings who are
present.

The open-minded traveller will usually see something straight away.
Some see lights and colours, others see actual people in both worlds.
The less clear-minded may see nothing at all at first but may
experience sensations as they are moved about by the Guides.

Then, the Guide will ask the traveller to describe him and his
clothing. At this point, if stable and happy to continue, he will be
lifted up through the floors and roof of the building in which his
body is lying. At this juncture, it should be understood that, while

the mind is now separated from the physical body and is experiencing aspects of the spiritual world, it is still able to record body sensations and sounds. The messages from the Guide are being relayed through the astral traveller's physical ears to his now remote mind. This dual awareness is typical of a controlled, conducted astral travel.

The silver cord stretches out behind the spiritual being and is, apparently, of limitless extension. The so-called dead, permanently living in heaven, can always identify an incarnate being by the silver cord which, of course, they no longer possess.

Apprehension, trepidation and sometimes fear may be experienced by the beginner depending on his degree of understanding. No harm can possibly befall him because he is protected at all times by the Guides. There is absolutely no danger of the silver cord becoming broken while travelling in the astral for that would result in the death of the body and people are never programmed by their kharmas to die in this way. It would obviously not be prudent to attempt to exteriorise a seriously ill person unless he were an adept at astral travelling.

It can happen that a novice claims that every experience he is apparently having is the result of his own imagination. Of course, it is perfectly feasible for a person to imagine himself to be flying or gliding through the air like a bird but when the Guide reports that the novice has left his body and is standing behind it, then he is. If the novice now claims that he is only imagining it, he is wrong.

At first, it may be difficult for a person to tell the difference between the reality of the exterior and his own imagination. The reality improves with practice until one becomes certain that one is not imagining the experience.

There are ways of proving that two or more people have really travelled to the astral and have not imagined the trip or faked it. All astral travels should be recorded either on a tape recorder or by a scribe. When travellers are taken to the planes in heaven without the others' knowledge, they see exactly the same things without being prompted and this is proof that the permanent objects on the planes are there for all to see and that the travellers are really seeing them.

Beginners are required to state during astral travel training exactly what they experience and nothing more. If they see nothing but blackness, they should say so. With increased understanding and spiritual awareness, the psychic ability of the aspirant is enhanced and his reality becomes stronger after each successive venture into the astral.

Those who succeed in being taken to the higher planes, Plane Four for example, invariably declaim that all colours are brighter, that the sky is brilliant but there is no sun and that they feel so free and elated. When told that they must return to their bodies, they exhibit a marked reluctance to do so because descending from Plane Four to the earth plane is an extremely depressing experience.

Returning to a heavy, sometimes aching or weary body is an unpleasant anticlimax after knowing the sheer joy of existing on the higher planes. The reward for having sampled the future delights of heaven is the knowledge that there is no death and that people can, after a rather frustrating and disappointing life on earth, continue to learn and progress to a state of happiness quite unattainable while incarnate.

There is a sixth method of astral travelling whereby the traveller, after prior agreement with a High Spiritual Being, is taken solo, that is to say, without a person acting as Relay. In this case there are two Guides who conduct the person to the astral. This method is only recommended to adepts who have a perfect understanding of what is happening to them, who have a very strong reality on the spiritual world and who are able to communicate with accuracy and facility.

One should not attempt to astral travel when unduly tired because perception will be inhibited. Drugs or alcohol are not necessary in order to induce exteriorisation and, should a person succeed in leaving his body while under the influence of either, he may experience hallucinatory visions.

After considerable practice at communication by spirit writing followed by astral travelling experience, the learner should find that his psychic perception is becoming considerably enhanced to the point where he can actually see spiritual beings in the room with him and can describe their wearing apparel and their movements. One sees psychically with the eyes of the spiritual body which are not subject to the physiological limitations that affect the physical eyes.

In order to achieve really good perception and a highly developed psychic awareness, it is essential to raise one's understanding to the point where one can accept, totally, and without the slightest doubt or scepticism the existence of the spiritual universe and the people in it. There exist beyond the earth plane realms of incredible beauty, bathed in a perpetual brilliant light, populated by beautiful, honest, ethical, loving people. These realms can be visited by the sincere, dedicated seeker who has a deep and earnest desire to find out the truth about his future life after the death of his body. In order to take up residence on a high plane, there is only one qualification necessary and that is spiritual height achieved by atoning for crimes committed in present and past lives. Service to others is one certain way of wiping out kharmic debts.

When, finally, the debts have been paid in full, the rewards of existence on a high plane in heaven are unimaginable to an incarnate person. Suffice it to say that the ultimate aim of every spiritual being is to quit the punishment planet, earth, for the last time and remain for eternity in the timeless, beautiful, peaceful surroundings in heaven that reflect the high state of mind of its inhabitants, there to continue to work for the benefit of others while savouring the tremendous inner tranquillity that is normal among the celestial élite.

CHAPTER TWELVE

THE PRINCIPLES OF KHARMA AND REINCARNATION

Kharma is defined as the life pattern planned for us before birth and is a basic guide, impressed upon the subconscious mind, that influences our fate or destiny.

Every spiritual being, before incarnation, is programmed to follow a certain way of life. The child who has a compelling instinct to become a musician, artist, engineer or actor or to follow any other demanding profession, is merely following his kharma. The blueprint is drawn before birth and has no connection with genetic descendancy other than the fact that the would-be athlete, for example, must incarnate into a suitable physical body in order to achieve any abilities in athletics. Similarly, a man programmed to become a wrestler would need a suitably fit and strong body to fulfil his kharma.

A spiritual being can be incarnated into any kind of cellular organism from an amoeba upwards. Therefore, during his spiritual development, a person may have been insect, animal, bird, fish or human. Although animals also have kharmas, it is not until the spiritual being takes on human bodies that kharma appears to be very significant.

The first law of kharma is very simple. You will reap as you sow. You will be treated as well or badly as you have treated others. Every bad deed has to be atoned for and every good deed will be rewarded. This law applies to every individual and cannot be by-passed. Your kharma covers not only your present life but many lifetimes and you may be atoning now for a crime committed many centuries ago in a different physical body.

What is atonement? It is the expiation of a crime or sin and can be completed in two basic ways; by suffering to the extent that you have caused others to suffer or by performing good work and giving service to your fellow men and women and total environment.

No sin is ever forgiven! This second law of kharma is entirely contrary to the teachings of the Christian churches whose dogma insists that an apology to God accompanied by suitable contrition automatically ensures absolution from guilt and responsibility.

It does not!

How often have you heard people say, "Why should it happen to her, she never did anyone any harm?" Perhaps the person concerned is suffering from a dreaded disease or suffers financial hardship or even marital distress. If you knew for what that person was atoning, you would understand and might even think that she was being let off lightly. When you look around at the misery in the world today just consider that you almost certainly contributed to the present situation by your behaviour in previous lives.

The perpetrators of the massacre of six million Jews and the atrocities committed in concentration camps in the second world war alone would account for a large amount of suffering in present time among people who have been reincarnated in order to atone for those

crimes.   People generally suffer as a retribution for earlier crimes
but, unfortunately, some suffer unnecessarily as a result of treatment
meted out to them by suppressive, ignorant or stupid people.

Only spiritual beings with kharma outstanding are reincarnated,
except in the case of High Spiritual Beings like Jesus Christ who was
reincarnated from Plane Five.   When, ultimately, the slate is wiped
clean by atoning for all previous crimes, one remains on a high plane
in heaven and reaps rich rewards in terms of peace of mind. One knows
the ultimate in joy,   for there can be far more joy experienced after
death than ever before it.

The earth, then, is the punishment planet and, apart from the
extreme rarity of a reincarnation for a special purpose, such as that
of Jesus Christ Who had completed His kharma before His birth, we are
all here to atone. This accounts for the fact that when several
people are suffering from exactly the same disease,   some may respond
to medical treatment and others may not.   Even spiritual healers,
extremely effective though they frequently are,   have their failures.
These are explained by the fact that if it is not in a person's kharma
to be healed, then he will not be.

The phenomenon of Lourdes is explained in the same way.   Thousands
make the pilgrimage to the religious centre every year but only
occasionally does someone receive a so-called miracle cure. The
remainder must continue to suffer in order to atone.   These healings,
incidentally, have nothing whatever to do with faith or the religious
beliefs or lack of them of the individual. Only those who have atoned
sufficiently will find that their kharma permits them to be healed.

The time span, measured in earth terms, of a spiritual being's
progress to the point of no return, namely Plane Five in heaven, is of
the order of many millions of years.   The earliest incarnations may
have occurred on other planets in other galaxies, and then a series of
lives on earth will have ensued.

The following actual kharmas were revealed by access to the Akashic
Record and by recall methods and are typical examples.

Our particular entity was born, after many previous lives, an
Egyptian in the first century A.D.   After attaining adulthood, he
studied astrology and became a "wizard" who told people's fortunes and
advised high officials as to what political courses they should take.
After overstepping the mark and treading on a few political toes,   he
was forced to flee the country.   He sailed to Italy where he set up a
magnificent home with servants in Pompeii.

In an attempt to possess the daughter of another man, Arbaces, the
Egyptian, murdered him by stabbing him in the back in a dark street at
night.   He then accused another man of the murder.   This fellow was
arrested and sentenced to fight in the gladiatorial arena in Pompeii
against lions which would undoubtedly have killed him.

Arbaces visited the arena but, before the accused man was forced to
fight the lions, Arbaces was denounced publicly as the murderer.
During the ensuing arguments, the towering pinnacle of Vesuvius began
to erupt, presaging the destruction of Pompeii. The Egyptian failed to
warn his colleagues to evacuate the city although he had been given
sufficient warning himself. Then, the molten lava filled the streets,
the searing hot volcanic ash pervaded the already oppressive

atmosphere and buildings began to topple as fissures appeared in the earth.   Arbaces, while hastening to escape, was crushed to death by a stone column which fell onto his head.

Apart from numerous minor anti-social acts,   Arbaces had committed murder which automatically ensures a further incarnation and had given false testimony in an attempt to have another man put to death for a crime that he did not commit.   Furthermore, he failed to save the lives of some important city officials when he had the opportunity to do so.   There were also sexual excesses with various women and all of these crimes had to be atoned for.

Several more incarnations followed until, in the fifteenth century, the same spiritual being who had been Arbaces was reincarnated as an Irishman and became a judge sitting with a tribunal. In this capacity, he was fair and just but then he was appointed governor of a prison and his sense of humanity seemed to desert him.   He developed a habit of putting prisoners into their dungeons without clothing and, in Ireland's climate, it was not long before they died of exposure or even froze to death.   This behaviour earned our subject more adverse kharma which was eventually atoned for as will be seen.

In the reign of Queen Elizabeth I, the same entity became a gunner in the English navy and, during a sea battle, his ship, the last in the line, was set afire and in order to escape the flames, he jumped overboard and, after swimming with no chance of being picked up,   he drowned.

In 1790, the spiritual being who was once Arbaces the Egyptian was a French nobleman but, owing to dishonesty with financial transactions he was sentenced to death in a Parisian court and beheaded with an axe.

Yet another birth in Athens in 1893 resulted in a further incarnation for the purposes of atonement and the young man of twenty-one, recently married and a tailor by trade, was caught up in the first world war and taken prisoner by the Germans.   He was trying to escape from the prison camp at the Tiergarten in Berlin where he and his comrades were kept starving in freezing conditions and he froze to death while waiting to cross a railway line.

This incident, coupled with further atonement by suffering from the cold during most of his present life were retribution for the crimes committed as an Irish prison governor.

The preceding paragraphs describe only a very small part of the kharma of one person.

A woman wondered why she had had to endure eight major operations, one of them without an anaesthetic. Her Akashic record showed that, in her previous life, she had been a Chinese woman doctor with a deplorable habit of operating on people while using no anaesthetic. This kind of poetic justice is a perfect example of atonement.

Yet another English woman suffered an extremely painful and protracted illness before dying from it. Her record showed that in her previous life she was a man. He drove a horse-drawn omnibus in Manhattan at around the turn of the century. An habitual drunkard, he was remonstrated with by a woman passenger for being intoxicated while driving his omnibus. He struck the woman so hard with the stock of his horse whip that he broke her jaw. He left his wife and two children virtually penniless while he indulged his craving for drink. His family suffered hunger and great hardship. The man finally died of alcohol poisoning at the incredibly early age of twenty-nine years. The decision to reincarnate as a woman was taken in order to give the entity a better opportunity of displaying gentleness. The latest incarnation was very successful in terms of atonement but the suffering was essential in order to wipe out the kharmic debt incurred in the previous life.

Terrorists, mass murderers, assassins and others who cause havoc on earth are frequently reincarnated into the animal world. Eventually, they can climb back to the human stage of evolution but only after considerable atonement.

Suicides are automatically reincarnated very soon after taking their lives to face exactly similar problems again so, far from escaping their situations, they only create worse ones for themselves. Taking one's own life is a very foolish thing to do as it cannot possibly bring any advantage to the individual, only greater hardship in a future existence.

What kinds of incarnate persons are likely to die, never to return to earth, having completed their kharmas? Typical examples are William Shakespeare, Isaac Newton, Albert Schweitzer, Albert Einstein, Ludwig van Beethoven and Florence Nightingale, all of whom are happy on the higher planes.

They all benefitted mankind while suffering to some degree themselves. Beethoven's deafness is one example of suffering while creating beautiful music that will soothe the ears of people for centuries to come. What worse affliction could a great musician suffer than the inability to hear the results of his own artistic creation?

Each one of these well-known benefactors devoted his or her life to serving mankind. They are all now reaping great rewards. One does not have to be famous to complete one's kharma and these are just a few of the more obviously deserving people who will never return.

Since the highest spiritual state normally attainable on earth is equivalent to Plane Four, in order to rise to Planes Five or Six, the entity after death must study hard and qualify in terms of his understanding of spiritual matters, his ethical standards and the degree to which he is altruistic.

The perspicacious reader will ask why most people do not recall their earlier lives or their existence in heaven. This is because, at birth, the contents of the subconscious mind are suppressed in such a way that recall is prevented. It would be difficult for most people to live their present life if they remembered what they had done before.

Sometimes a Plane Four entity is reincarnated and retains memories of his existence in heaven, for what purpose he has returned to earth, and he may even recall earlier lives. These cases are not so rare as one might think but, because any child that talks about subjects that are not understood by adults is told that he is imagining things, the memories fade and are forgotten by the time the child leaves school.

"Every one knows that we only live once!" This platitude, entirely false, is responsible for much lack of understanding.

It will not have escaped the notice of the observant reader that the short list of High Spiritual Beings mentioned earlier did not contain the names of any religious people. This is because those who follow or preach a dogmatic religion have to accept the tenets of that belief completely. Once they have done this, their minds are closed and they can never learn the truth.

Albert Schweitzer's is an exceptional case in that he was an ardent seeker of the truth and, although an active participant in religious life, he came to the realisation that the so-called Christian truths bore little resemblance to historical fact. He even went so far as to accuse the church of being evasive and of distorting or suppressing facts whenever it was confronted by embarrassing evidence that tended to contradict its own ideas of the truth.

After his return to heaven, Plane Four, in fact, Albert was told the truth and, because of his open and enquiring mind, he was not only willing but able to reject his preconceptions where they differed from the facts. This attitude enabled him to rise to Plane Five very soon after his re-arrival in heaven. After further periods of intensive study, Albert Schweitzer qualified both spiritually and intellectually to reside on Plane Six.

Only a state of high ethical standards and moral virtues with total acceptance of responsibility by the individual will ever lead the peoples of earth towards the paradise about which so many of them dream. The future of every person lies with himself!

Clearly, the message is this. If you want to set back your kharma and delay your ultimate happiness indefinitely, remain apathetic towards life, work and the welfare of others. If, on the other hand, you wish to wipe out your unsavoury past and enjoy the indescribable wonders and beauty of the higher planes in a state of elation for eternity, then you must turn your attention outwards and acquire the positive characteristics that lead to a highly successful incarnation, thus releasing you from the suffering that life after life on the punishment planet involves.

Since no birth is an accident, why are some babies born crippled, spastic, autistic, deaf, blind and so on? Kharma!

A girl in the Midlands of England in the nineteenth century who indulged in numerous clandestine sexual exploits and who gave birth to three babies, each of which she smothered and disposed of, was born in 1933 with spina bifida to suffer five years of sheer misery at a time when the medical profession could do nothing for her. Yet another case is known of a negress who murdered her twins in a particularly horrible manner. She was reincarnated as a cat.

Whatever our kharmas may be, we are here to make the most of them. The negative approach to life is self-destructive. A woman who lived in a cottage and did nothing much but make tea in her silver teapot carried on doing the same thing after she passed on, until a spiritual being pointed out to her that there are more things to existence than those of which she was aware.

Materialists, after death, are often unaware that they have died. So immersed in their individual, mundane existences have they become, that this is their state of mind which, of course, transcends the death of the body. The spiritually-minded are soon aware that the beauty around them is familiar and that *here* is where they belong.

CHAPTER THIRTEEN

THE PROOF OF RECALL

Proof of reincarnation, as of most other spiritual facts, remains a subjective experience. The truth is not demonstrable but it is knowable. As an example, if witnesses to an act of levitation were asked if it proved anything to them, what would they say? It would make a different impression on each witness depending on their knowledge and understanding.

At the best, the act of levitation, occurring before their own eyes in the company of others who admitted to seeing the same event, would indicate that there was something taking place that they could not explain by resorting to "rational scientific explanation".

The Buddhist monk, able to levitate, would ascribe his ability to years of ascetic training and a lifetime of meditation. The materialist would start searching for hidden wires but the event itself, although observed and confirmed by a number of onlookers, would prove nothing. So it is with reincarnation. Although hypnotic regression is commonplace and subjects repeatedly appear to revert to incidents in earlier lives, the "cognoscenti" talk of cryptomnesia and go to great lengths to explain that all such incidents are the result of a dramatisation of events portrayed in books or stories told in childhood but long since forgotten.

To the psychologist who believes that the mind is the brain, memory of past lives is impossible, and here he or she will go to great lengths to explain, unless such a memory had been inherited genetically. He will talk of memory cells and DNA and a variety of other physical entities, stretching his own imagination further than he would have to if he were to accept them, in order to avoid an understanding of spiritual factors.

No amount of genuine corroborative evidence will convince the materialistically-minded critic that reincarnation is a fact. He will always put up a counter-argument based on an entire lack of knowledge and a dearth of understanding of the subject. Those who know least about the spiritual truths of man's existence fight the hardest to deny others the privilege of access to that realm of experience and comprehension that they themselves are unwilling to contemplate, partly through personal fear of their own past and partly through a deep-rooted desire to conform with the agreed-upon rules of their particular professional disciplines.

It takes a courageous person to speak out with conviction against the tenets and dogmas of his own profession because he knows that he will have to face denigration, ridicule, censure and sometimes even disciplinary action within his specific, esoteric society.

The proof, then, of the realities of the spiritual existence is likely to remain a matter of individual, inner awakening and realisation.

I have recalled incidents form a number of my former lives by different techniques but, unlike some people whose past is forced upon them, perhaps in dreams or merely by an intense feeling or a strong memory, I have had to delve deeply into my spiritual history in order to obtain my own proof of earlier incarnations.

Originally, I discovered an ability to recall incidents from my entire incarnation record. Later, after working with my very highly-placed Guides on the other side, I was given recalls by direct telepathy. The Guide would first visit the Akashic Record in the Great Hall of Memories and study my past. He would then return and project the scenes and dialogue into my mind, with my full co-operation and awareness, while I was wide awake.

By far the most impressive means of re-experiencing one's earlier lives is by astral travelling to the Great Hall on Plane Four and seeing the Akashic Record directly, just as all spiritual beings have to do after they return to heaven from an incarnation. If the scenes unfolding before one's eyes take on an horrific aspect, as they frequently do, one relives the incidents, now knowing with certainty of the past guilt and longing to get up and run from the hall.

There is no escape, however. Tears of remorse may pour from the eyes and a shivering, shaking and trembling may take over the whole body as the stark truth of one's former vile crimes is laid at one's feet. The emotional shock of realisation and recall strikes deeply to the mind and the head sags to the chest in silence.

When the terrifying scenario being re-enacted finally fades from the screen, the perpetrator remains stunned, unable to understand how he or she could ever have committed such atrocities. Denial is not only impossible but unnecessary because the guilty person knows with certitude the wickedness of his transgressions and is infused with culpability.

Before the Akashic Record, the braggart is bereft of contumely and hubris is transmuted into mortification. The leavening effect of having the soul bared for all to see is often startling and the sight of a self-assured, vainglorious individual deflating with a severe attack of remorse is an edifying experience.

Amanda and I have trained a number of people in astral travelling and when they can visit the Akashic Record themselves they *have* the proof that they have been seeking regarding reincarnation. Only very strong realities gained by direct recall, projected telepathic recall or reviewing the Akashic Record will furnish the *proof* of rein-carnation to the individual. Others may accept it and believe it but gnosis can only succeed personal experience.

An outstanding example of the proof of recall occurred when one of our students was given a recall, in my absence, of his earlier life as a Roman officer. Unknown to him, his recall was, incident for incident, identical with one that I had been given months earlier in which I, too, was a Roman officer. It appeared that we were fellow officers in the Legion and we rode on horse-back, side-by-side, on our return from a successful campaign, about the year 2 A.D. The student's description of our commander, the tumultuous reception in Rome, the troops marching behind us and our ultimate departure to the fields to bivouac and eat, all tallied exactly with my recall received months earlier. Why not? We were both there!

A further remarkable revelation occurred while Amanda and I were checking the last life of one of our trainees. He had been present, in his former body, at Eindhoven in Holland on January 1st, 1945 when the RAF airfield was attacked by thirty Messerschmitt 109's and Focke-Wulf 190's. This raid was the most traumatic experience of my present life and the twenty-one minutes duration seemed to last a whole day.   Our airmen suffered many casualties and we lost numerous aircraft on the ground. Among the casualties was a fellow corporal in the Signals Echelon.   This poor chap had his right foot severed at the ankle by a twenty-millimetre cannon shell as he lay on the floor of a hut. He was taken to 51 Mobile Field Hospital and I heard no more of him. Having, since the war, always imagined that my erstwhile colleague would have been given an artificial foot and returned home to a normal life, I was astounded to discover, when his Akashic Record was disclosed, that he had died, shortly after the incident, of gangrene.

Yet, here he was again sitting next to me in a new body. Intrigued, I delved into my wartime photographs and found one in which he, a Flight Sergeant and I were taken together. Amazingly, there was a strong resemblance between the young man in the photograph and the one by my side. This, apparently, is to be expected because of the influence of the spiritual features upon the physical body. This event showed that, in one lifetime, one may know another person in more than one physical body.

CHAPTER FOURTEEN

COMMUNICATION WITH THE SPIRITUAL WORLD

Communication with and from the spiritual world has been going on for thousands of years and the bible contains hundreds of references to it. It was not until the nineteenth century that mediums began to produce phenomena so startling that even some of the scientists of the day took it upon themselves to investigate them. As late as the eighteenth century, any female person claiming to be able to communicate with the spiritual world was burned at the stake as a witch, usually with the wholehearted connivance of church ministers.

Although the witchcraft act had not been repealed in the nineteenth century, public opinion had swung to a more tolerant attitude and people were no longer judicially murdered for being psychic. Such eminent scientists as Sir William Crookes, Sir Oliver Lodge, Cromwell Varley and Dr Maxwell set out to investigate occult phenomena with every intention of exposing them as fraudulent but they all concluded their investigations by being totally convinced of the spiritual nature of the phenomena which defied description by the scientific knowledge of the time.

There are always a few unscrupulous people prepared to jump onto any band wagon that trundles past and the subject that became known as spiritualism was, unfortunately, exploited by a minority of fakers. Many were exposed and this left the already sceptical public with a general feeling that mediums, psychics and spiritualists were all either corrupt opportunists or were very misguided and gullible.

There is a type of person who is attracted to mystical subjects for the wrong reasons. The very mystery excites them but these types rarely learn much because they are not true seekers.

Thousands of bereaved people have, through mediums, received confirmation of the continued existence after death by communicating with their loved ones who had passed on.

In the minds of the general public, anything to do with communication with the dead is spooky, taboo or even dangerous. Then, of course, there are the religious who believe that it is the work of the devil. It is not really surprising that these attitudes are held by numbers of people because spiritual séances are usually reported as taking place in darkened rooms with the sitters holding hands, trumpets floating around the room, diaphonous wisps of ectoplasm manifesting themselves, materialisations of bodies or parts of bodies, table rapping, sepulchral voices emanating from space and objects moving about apparently without human agency.

While all of these phenomena do occur and have been substantiated by numerous eminent citizens with no axe to grind, communication with the spiritual world, when conducted with spiritual beings who have a good understanding and are highly spiritual, may be effected anywhere, in any conditions of light or dark, at any time and entirely without apparatus of any kind.

While driving my car, flying my aeroplane, as a passenger in an aircraft, or just lying in bed, I am able to communicate with those on the other side of the veil. Because I always know with whom I am communicating, I do not need to resort to the hit and miss method practised by some of saying, "Is there anyone there?" I always know who is there because I see them in my presence through my psychic vision. Furthermore, since spirit writing is out of the question while driving a car or flying an aircraft, for example, I have developed a special method of communication.

Owing to the need for a would-be communicant to have a thorough understanding of the laws governing such communication, I am not at liberty to disclose the method in this book. The subject is fully covered in my book, "How to Talk with the Dead".

Because, previously, the principles have never been understood, communication with those in heaven has remained an esoteric art practised only by those especially gifted with psychic awareness and mediumistic abilities.

Remember, spiritual beings know what you are thinking, whether you are aware of their presence or not. Additionally, unlike most incarnate people, they know the real meaning behind your words because they receive your concepts, and are not misled if your choice of words is inappropriate or inadequate.

Communication between spiritual beings in heaven is almost invariably on a basis of mutual understanding because concepts are telepathically exchanged and one's aura reacts if one is in any way mendacious. Thus, the liar can achieve nothing for he cannot hide his intentions.

Books and documents are written in concept writing which has the appearance of shorthand. Any spiritual being is able to read concept writing automatically and without training but he will not understand it if the concepts expressed are beyond his comprehension.

No matter what language a spiritual being spoke while incarnate, he can communicate with people on earth of any nationality because conceptual thought does not involve words or language. This is why concept writing cannot be translated word for word into any earth language and philologists would be wasting their time in attempting it.

During the study and practice of communication with the spiritual world, one should be constantly on one's guard against low spiritual beings on the other side who may be out for a bit of fun, as they see it. Some of them will deliver false messages and generally lead the inexperienced communicator up the garden path. This is why it is of vital importance to know with whom one is dealing.

Low spiritual beings will never attempt to interfere with a genuine communication in the presence of High Spiritual Beings because they fear them. Those in authority on the higher planes are able to command low spiritual beings to leave the environment or, if required, order them to be present to account for themselves.

Those who attempt to communicate with the spiritual world just for "fun" may be invoking a reaction that might surprise them or, in some cases, even horrify them. The secret is *never* to meddle with something that you do not understand and always to approach the subject with a discreet reverence. All High Spiritual Beings behave in an exemplary manner. The ladies curtsy and the gentlemen bow when greeting one another. Their normal human characteristics are still present and the person renowned for a strong sense of humour on earth will still retain it in heaven.

One may laugh and joke with one's communicants, in an inoffensive manner, of course, but the dedicated seeker after knowledge should approach the prospect of learning the truth from those who are the custodians of it, namely, High Spiritual Beings, with an attitude of respect.

If, at any time, the messages received seem malicious, or foretell unpleasantness, the session should be terminated at once. In the event of persistent low standards of communication, the incarnate communicant should refrain from further attempts as it is obvious that his understanding is not sufficiently developed and he may become deeply involved in a situation that he cannot handle, by attracting low spiritual beings.

Nothing is ever given away to people on earth by God or the spiritual world. Everything has to be earned the hard way, by intensive study and by exemplary behaviour. This applies equally well to acquiring the skills of psychic communication.

Some mediums, who have considerable abilities, often limit their own progress because they harbour the negative emotion of jealousy when confronted by another, more capable medium and are unwilling to learn from him or her.

There is no limit imposed on anyone from without. All limitations in the psychic field are either self-imposed or endogenous. A deep, inner drive to seek the answers to life and existence, coupled with a purposeful dedication to study and a total willingness to confront one's faults and errors will, ineluctably, attract the desired benefits and rewards.

Everyone capable of sustained, intellectual activity should ponder deeply every day upon the subject of metaphysics, for knowledge is denied those who do not seek it.

CHAPTER FIFTEEN

POSTHUMOUS SCRIPTS

There follow a few of the many scripts that have been written through my mind and hand by High Spiritual Beings now enjoying their existence on the highest planes in heaven.

I am Leonardo da Vinci writing through Alan Valiant. Good evening to you. It gives me great pleasure to be invited to speak to you. At present I am on Plane Six working as a consultant to the Gardeners of the Earth with whom I communicate through God Whom I know well.

The relationships between earth scientists and the spiritual world are my main interest. In the fifteenth century, I was sculptor, painter, engineer, mathematician, scientist, astronomer, inventor, military advisor and professor of languages, Latin, Italian and French.

The church was my greatest enemy. They, in their abysmal ignorance, countered every new theory that I put forward. They knew better! I have had the last laugh since I "died", though. The priests who tortured and killed people for not believing what *they* did have had to pay a terrible price for their crimes committed in the name of God.

I, Leonardo da Vinci, tell you that religions are the *curse* of mankind and that the truth must be brought to the men and women of religion before they ruin the world completely.

Man's spiritual progress must not be impeded any longer by the ignorance of the clergy. The more deeply religious, in the church sense, the lower one's spiritual height! You cannot reach the higher planes in heaven unless you drop everything you have been taught about religions.

During my last incarnation, I lived under a hagiarchy whose power was total over the citizen. Anyone who dared to challenge the authority of the church was punished cruelly and thousands were executed.

In order to ensure my own security so that I could carry out the work that I instinctively knew I had been born to do, I suffered religion in silence but never, after the age of about fifteen years, did I accept it. Perhaps it was wrong of me to fail to express my true feelings but I knew that, if I had, I would have been tortured and possibly murdered by the priests.

Devoted entirely to my work in all its great variety, I pretended, right up until my "death", to show allegiance to the church. After my return to heaven, I saw in the Akashic Record the frightful atrocities that were committed in the name of God and I was glad that I did not expose myself to the appalling ignorance of the custodians of the Christian religion.

Now that I am on Plane Six in heaven, I know the truth and please believe me when I tell you with the greatest sincerity that, here, religion is meaningless and non-existent. The Christian religions are mythological, based as they are upon erroneous beliefs. It may be observed that those on earth who are the most evolved spiritually have the least to do with religions. I hope that these few words have clarified my true position, as it was then and as it is now.

Good evening to you. This is Thomas Alva Edison writing to you. My abilities as an inventor are well-known throughout the world but I should like to say, in the first place, that all of the ideas that I developed were put into my mind by two High Spiritual Beings on Plane Six. They were asked to stay with me all my life and feed me ideas telepathically. One of them was a clever inventor of the seventeenth century in America. His name was Peter Carstairs and he invented mechanical devices and general engineering improvements. Unfortunately he never received publicity for his great work.

The other High Spiritual Being is a lady who is Peter's soul-mate. They lived in my house and laboratory, without my knowledge, of course. Apparently, I more than justified myself and produced many more inventions than they expected me to.

I was residing on Plane Three before my last incarnation, when I was told that there was a great need for technical improvements on earth to enhance the basic living standards of millions of people. On being approached by a High Spiritual Being, I was asked if I would like to consider this very important incarnation. After further discussion and a close study of the Record of Probabilities, I agreed. There would be great help available to me at all times from the spiritual world, I was informed.

One of the factors that made me decide to accept the challenge was that I was told that, if my mission were successful, it would be my final incarnation.

My mother was very carefully selected and it was she who finally educated me because my teachers gave up trying, thinking I was stupid whereas, in fact, I knew far more than they did.

I worked up to twenty hours a day and my laboratory workers kept the jobs going twenty-four hours a day. Although my invention of the phonograph was a fascinating experience, my favourite invention is the incandescent electric lamp. We had only candles and oil lamps and gas lighting in the streets and, after dark, it was so dismal everywhere that I decided to do something about it. When I switched on the city lights for the first time, it was a tremendous thrill and one that I can even now recall.

Born of Dutch immigrants who were quakers, I was put off religion at an early age, thank God! If I had believed the ridiculous ideas that they asked me to believe, I would never have achieved anything worth while.

Religions are the curse of the earth. Sweep away *belief* and substitute *knowledge* and you will see the earth illuminated by a brilliance of understanding that will surpass the greatest effects of all the incandescent lamps in the world today.

This is Charles Darwin, author of "The Origin of Species" and many other works on biology and animal life writing through Alan Valiant. I hereby admit that, since I "died", I have discovered that my theories concerning the origins of man were wrong. There is no missing link on earth between the primeval life in the sea, where animal life began on earth, and man because man was introduced to earth from the planet Yolland Allicay and has no terrestrial, antecedent animal forms. Also, my theory of natural selection, although plausible to many scientists, was also incorrect.

I now know that all animal behaviour is controlled by High Spiritual Beings in heaven. God can cause mutations or modify the chromosomic or genetic structure in any animal life, at will. I was never, contrary to the beliefs of some, religious, but was very much spiritually inclined.

Also, I now know that the enigmas of the homing pigeon, the eel, the salmon and whale and squid mating migrations are explained by the fact that High Spiritual Beings in heaven guide and influence the creatures to perpetuate their species. I freely admit that I failed to appreciate, adequately, the true significance of the spiritual existence while I was incarnate. I beseech all researchers in biology and allied disciplines to study spiritual subjects concurrently with their major subjects. They will be pleasantly surprised at that which they learn.

It has been observed by many modern palaeontologists that my theory of natural selection does not appear to be supported by the remains of ancient species, the fossils or skeletons of which are still being discovered. These observations are correct. It is God Who, at appropriate moments in time, alters instantaneously, the genetic programme for future species.

Man has already discovered how to do this himself but, whereas he creates the effects by physical manipulation of DNA, God, using spiritual control, is able to achieve any desired change so that all future forms of that particular species will be different from their predecessors.

I still follow closely the progress of man's scientific investigations into the origins of species and feel certain that, if only they could acquire an understanding of the spiritual influences on both themselves and the fauna of the world, they would advance in leaps and bounds.

This is Oliver Lodge writing through Alan Valiant. Good evening to you. I was a scientist in England during my last life and did a great deal of development work on wireless sets, beginning with spark telegraphy and later developing valve transmitters and receivers.

I became interested in spiritual matters after seeing Daniel Home producing phenomenal effects such as tables and chairs moving violently, apparently of their own volition. He could also levitate very easily. So convinced was I by Home's demonstrations that I began a long and systematic series of investigations into spiritualism and the occult.

My book, "My Philosophy", was partly based on my knowledge of spiritual matters and partly on my own observations. Actually my philosophy was not very accurate and was, largely, guesswork. I was knighted for my work on wireless and allied subjects and for my contribution to science.

Since I "died", I have worked my way up from Plane Two to Plane Six where I now work with other, more eminent, philosophers. I also work with scientists and help people who are due for reincarnation to understand the the technology that it is hoped they will be using, while incarnate. You see, spiritual beings do not arrive on earth as

94

babies knowing nothing. They need to have considerable knowledge before they are born, if they are to perform useful work. Not all re-incarnated beings are given prior training for their lives to come but those who are destined to perform great duties invariably are.

Heaven is a better place than earth, the punishment planet. I have had fourteen lives but I do not want to reincarnate and should not have to. There is so much of interest here. Everyone on this plane is very happy and friendly and there is love everywhere. Only the most intellectual beings, who are also extremely able, reach this plane but their ability must be proved to have been for mankind's benefit.

CHAPTER SIXTEEN

THE FINAL CONFESSION

The script that follows was written, at Amanda's request, some considerable time after our first meeting with an ex-pope.* He appeared in our room dressed in full papal regalia but we could see immediately that he was a very unhappy man. Subsequent questioning showed that he was totally confused, even angry. He hung his head and was obviously in a state of considerable embarrassment engendered by his disillusionment concerning his most recent rôle on earth. The ex-pope was asked to study the truth from then on, which he assured us he would do.

Many months later, he asked our spiritual advisors for a further interview. He was granted permission and, again, he arrived wearing his papal robes. This surprised us greatly because he had previously assured us that he would not continue to wear them. However, after greeting Amanda and me courteously, he suddenly removed his robes of papal office and, symbolically, threw them onto the floor at his feet, remaining standing, bare-headed, clad only in a plain white spiritual robe.

After this demonstration of his acceptance of the futility of his religious life, the ex-pope agreed to write through me in the hope that he may be able to prevent others with similar religious aspirations from falling into the same trap as he did.

April 27th, 1980

This is ex-pope* writing through Mr Alan Valiant, a highly spiritual medium. Upon my return to heaven when I died, I was distressed to discover that my last incarnation as a priest and, finally, as pope of the Catholic Church, was a total waste of my life and the lives of many others.

At the time of my death, I believed that which I had been taught, namely, that the pope was the spiritual head of God's church and was, therefore, God's representative on earth. Furthermore, my own vanity was burnished to a high degree by all the pomp, ceremony and ritual that surrounded my high office. The result was that I had acquired a completely false concept of myself as a man and, instead of being spiritually pure, I was anything but pure.

The façade that I showed my colleagues and the catholic public was, I can see now, merely an expression of my vanity because, within, I was really conscious of the great power vested in me by the Church elders and I must admit to a kind of gloating and self-praise.

On awaking in heaven and being told that I had died, at first I could not believe it. Then, when I realised that I had, I began to ask questions of the young lady who was looking after me in the reception quarters; such questions as, "When may I see God or Jesus Christ?" and "Do They know that I am here?" The shocking reply was to the effect that neither God nor Jesus Christ was interested in me because I was a low spiritual being. At this, I remonstrated, saying that I had given my life in the service of God and Christ, surely that meant something?

The very patient young lady gently explained, while I became more and more aggravated, that whatever I thought I had been on earth, here in heaven, I had no particular importance and certainly no status.

I am afraid I lost my temper many times with many people. I continued to wear my papal robes hoping to impress people here but they were not impressed in the least.

While I pondered on a lifetime of devotion to God and Jesus Christ apparently wasted, I was approached by spiritual beings who were obviously very high, spiritually. Their countenances radiated a beautiful golden light, as in the bible where angels are described. Their approach to me was of infinite tolerance and deep understanding with no hint of criticism.

While I fumed and raged in shocked confusion, they merely explained the true situation. I had become, they said, yet one more victim of the earth's false religions. They understood that my original motives in becoming a priest were genuine and based upon a strong, innate desire to assist people to rise, spiritually. Then, they went on to explain that, because the catholic religion, like all others, does not know the truth about God and Jesus Christ, that which I had taught and been taught was almost entirely false. This had resulted not only in my own spiritual regression but in the retardation of the spiritual advancement of millions of catholics. Thus, instead of rising and helping others to rise, I had achieved the exact opposite.

You may imagine how I felt. My vanity took some very hard knocks, I can assure you. Many readers of this, my first communication to peoples of earth since my death, may remark upon my refraining from the use of religious terminology. This is because, after many difficulties, I have learned the basic truths about God, Jesus Christ and life and death.

Although there are numerous spiritual beings on my plane in heaven, Plane One, who still practise Christianity, they do it more from habit than anything else and they are unwilling to learn the truth. So was I but, eventually, I realised that the only way that I could ever redeem myself was by discarding everything that catholicism had ever taught me and by studying the truth as contained in the numerous books in heaven and as taught by our instructors, here.

High Spiritual Beings do not talk in religious terms and, although I have not yet seen either God or Jesus Christ, I know that they are very different Beings when compared with the commonly-held beliefs of catholics and that neither of them wishes to be worshipped.

The forgiveness of sins, which is a major aspect of the catholic belief is, I have discovered, a myth. A sin cannot be pardoned or forgiven by anyone in heaven, including God. The only way in which a sin can be expiated is for the perpetrator of it to atone for it. This can only be achieved by suffering or by helping others in order to balance the kharmic debt.

Catholics, of course, are taught that to talk of reincarnation is heresy and that communication with the spiritual world is the work of the devil. I have learned that reincarnation is one of the *facts* of existence. We all have many lives without which we cannot rise, spiritually, so to call this fact heresy is a fundamental religious error. Also, although some people who attempt to communicate with the "other world" find themselves in deep water, it is only because, owing to their lack of understanding they become the victims of stupid or evil spiritual beings on the lower astral plane.

Communication, properly carried out by people on both sides of the veil who really understand what is happening, is neither caused by the devil, nor is it sinful. In the first place, the devil does *not* exist. This is another catholic myth exploded. Evil-minded spiritual beings exist in heaven as on earth and it is they who deliberately attempt to cause trouble in the same way as their incarnate counterparts do. The one reference in the bible concerning spiritism, upon which the catholic dogma concerning spiritual communication is based, is totally misleading and has no validity.

I, ex-pope*, am now in a position to state with total conviction and without fear of contradiction by High Spiritual Beings here that not one word in the bible was contributed by God, either directly or indirectly.

Christianity, a man-made religion, has misinterpreted almost every incident reported in the bible with the result that it cannot be regarded as a valid religion. Much of the bible reports true events, as they happened, but the inferences placed by priests and theologians upon the various happenings are, mostly, false.

Until I returned to heaven and read a book here that was written by the highest spiritual beings in the universe, I believed that the bible contained the truth and that I knew it. I was very wrong. As my mind was closed to free thought, about the occurrences described in the bible, and being able to accept only the dogma of my religion, I could never have known the truth. Many aspects of it have now been made manifest to me, and I can see how totally wrong are the religious views of most situations written about in the bible.

I no longer use the word "holy" because here, in heaven, it has no meaning. Although I prayed and led thousands of others in prayer to the "Holy Mother of God", I now know that Mary was not the mother of God because Jesus Christ is not, and was not, God. The myth of the virgin birth is another false tenet of Christianity and Christ's mother, although resident in heaven, has no particular status and never receives or answers prayers. Neither, I was amazed to learn, does Jesus Christ. Only God, Himself, receives prayers and either acts upon them or does not according to whether the supplicant deserves that for which he or she is praying.

It is with a heart heavy with regret that I write this, today. Regret that I was insufficiently spiritually aware to avoid the trap of religion, for that is what it is. It is an insidious snare that, unfortunately, brings within its meshes those who have the best of intentions and who sincerely believe that they are conforming with that which Jesus Christ wants them to do.

Jesus Christ is a great and wonderful man and is, I have been told, a very, very, High Spiritual Being and a great and wonderful man in heaven but he is ashamed of the blindness of men who persist in perpetuating the Christian religion in its many perverted forms. You can imagine my shock when I discovered that those who rise spiritually the highest while incarnate are those who do not become attached to

98

any religion but who follow the path of righteousness merely because they know it to be right. Their minds are free. They can evaluate their experiences without distortions creeping into their mental processes as invariably happens with religious people.

As only God receives prayers, the so-called saints of the catholic religion are not involved in answering them. I have been in heaven for a considerable time, now, and have not met a saint. The people who are revered as saints still exist, of course, because no person can cease to exist but, after their deaths, they would have been confronted by the same kind of situation as I was. There are no saints in heaven.

A person's worth in heaven is not dependent upon the results of a religious committee's findings after they have investigated his qualifications as a saint. One's status and value in heaven are determined by spiritual height, which in turn is determined by past behaviour and one's ability, knowledge and understanding. Therefore, no group of people on earth can possibly influence the status of a person who has passed on. Everything concerning that person's position in heaven has been decided and determined by the time of his passing.

In church, we call upon God to grant us His grace which really means, "look upon us with favour". What we do not realise is that God is impartial and never shows favour to anyone. Since we have free will our condition at any given time is the result of our own thinking and behaviour. "God's grace" is yet another myth. The law of kharma is immutable. Only if it were not could anyone receive favour because that is contrary to the first law, "You reap as you sow". Here then, is the sad fact that millions pray for and expect God's grace, never suspecting that their weekly presence in church and their persistent pleading are having absolutely no desirable elevatory effect upon their spiritual status.

You, and you alone, can save yourself! The *only* way that you can do this is to obey the laws of ethics and to strive to do good at all times. It is quite unrealistic to expect God or Jesus Christ to save us if we are not prepared to accept responsibility for our own condition and, in fact, They cannot and will not.

If all missionaries were to disconnect themselves from the practice of their religions and apply themselves solely to bringing succour to the needy, they would rise spiritually higher than those of their brethren who continued as before.

It is quite possible to try to follow the example set by Jesus Christ without ever becoming associated with, or involved in, religious practice. Christ's example will stand for ever as a testimony to His knowledge, ability, courage and spiritual importance.

For a considerable time, I have been undergoing intensive instruction by my three spiritual advisors. They are three gentlemen from Plane Four. Patiently, they explain the fallacies of religion and then they allow me to interview other spiritual beings who have finally eliminated their religious bias and who have reached Plane Four. In this way, I am gradually re-orientating my own viewpoints but I confess it is extremely difficult to rid myself of my religious beliefs although the truth has been explained to me.

Having succeeded in being able to accept teaching by others without my former arrogance and self-importance standing in my way, I feel that I am, at last, making good inroads into the complex and sometimes confusing subject of the study of spiritual truth. It is, of course, confusing to me only because of my numerous preconceptions, every one of which I must discard before I am able to know and fully understand the truth.

June 6th, 1982

I was asked to come here today to examine my foregoing script, in order to check that it is totally accurate and to state whether I wish to alter anything, in the light of my subsequent experience in heaven, or to remove from or add to the script. After re-examination with Mr Valiant, I decided that it is absolutely true and correct.

Since I returned to heaven, to the lower astral plane, in fact, I have taken stock of my own attitudes with the result that my former arrogance and anger have given way to a deep sense of humility, coupled with gratitude that, here at least, I can discover the Truth.

My childish attempts to gain respect by parading in my religious garments have long since given way to a meek approach whereby I wear a plain white robe and defer to all others, most particularly the High Spiritual Beings who know so much more than I do.

Only since I discarded my former false attitudes and exchanged bombast for humility, has anyone else taken a close interest in me. Now, I enjoy being taught by very learned men in heaven but they would not have attempted to help me as long as I clung to my former beliefs and continued to behave as I was doing.

By virtue of my change of outlook and my newly-acquired willingness to co-operate I have discovered, to my great relief and joy, that I have graduated spiritually to the upper astral plane. This has given me a strong stimulus to strive, even harder, to rise as high as possible before my next, inevitable, reincarnation.

I say to you dear people, do not expect to have to wait for the judgment day or to be raised from the dead. As soon as you die, you still exist and you will eventually judge yourselves, as I have done. The more I learn, here in heaven, the more I see the great harm that the Christian religions, in particular, are doing to the real spiritual welfare of their millions of followers.

There will be, no doubt, many pious and devout people who will rise up in anger at the invalidations of religions contained in this book but it is with the first law of kharma very much in mind that I write these words. For me to have falsified just one item of information in this work will have exposed me to a retribution such as few will ever have incurred.

If I have, deliberately, made any false statements about God or Jesus Christ, or made any claims without full and total justification, then I stand indicted and can expect a future atonement commensurate with the magnitude of my error.

By virtue of that which I teach, I would reap a most unpleasant harvest, having sown the seeds of calumny.

Because I know the sources of my information and am genuinely able to communicate with the Highermost, a fact to which several other people are able to testify, I have not the slightest hesitation in commending this work to those seeking True Enlightenment.

Both God and Christ would much prefer to see the churches turned into schools and the cathedrals converted into universities in all of which *the facts,* as opposed to *belief,* about one's existence should be a compulsory subject.

As long as religious thought predominates over the minds of men, spiritual progress will continue to be very slow. Only when the truth of their eternal existence is known and when they are totally aware of and able to abide by the laws of kharma will the peoples of earth begin to save themselves many more lifetimes of suffering, often to no avail.

There is more than enough evidence on earth of the spiritual existence if only people would study it. There are hundreds of books explaining it. The almost diurnal enigmas of spiritual origin are there to make you think, so please, my good people, *think!*

Universal apostasy is the highest aim of the spiritual hierarchy, for a knowledge of the Truth *must* be substituted for religious belief if the people of earth are ever to live their lives as God intends.

He who wields the broom of iconoclasm can only sweep away the ancient cobwebs of dogma by the light of the truth, otherwise he exposes himself to the ridicule and denigration of those whose convictions and faith adumbrate their innate perspicacity.